Are Your Ears Burning?

What Your Body Knows
Before You Do

By

Jason A. Solomon, B.Ed.

First Edition © 2025 Jason A. Solomon, B.Ed.

All rights reserved. This book is copyrighted. Except as permitted under the Australian Copyright Act, no part of this book may be reproduced or used in any form without written consent from the publisher.

The author asserts the moral right to be identified as the author of this work. This book blends research with original case studies. All characters, images, scenes and examples written for illustration are original. Any match with real people is coincidental.

Published by Aussie Guy's Books, Sydney, Australia
Printed on demand worldwide
ISBN 978-1-7642115-7-4
www.aussieguysbooks.com.au

Are Your Ears Burning?
What Your Body Knows Before You Do
Author: Jason A. Solomon, B.Ed.
Publisher: Aussie Guy's Books, Sydney, Australia
Imprint: Aussie Guy's Books
Printing: On demand, worldwide distribution
ISBN 978-1-7642115-7-4
www.aussieguysbooks.com.au

DISCLAIMER
This book provides general information about psychology, biology and human behaviour. It is not a substitute for professional medical, psychological or therapeutic advice. Readers should seek qualified support for personal health concerns. The publisher and author take no responsibility for decisions made based on the material in this book.

Contents

Preface 1

Where the Saying Really Comes From 5

When the Body Was an Omen 10

Case Study: 14

What a Burning Ear Actually Is 21

The Brain Hates Randomness 25

Experiments You Can Try 30

Why Humans Fear Being Talked About 39

The Social Alarm System 44

The Illusion of Feeling Mentioned 49

The Teacher Who Felt Watched 56

Turning Sensation Into Story 67

The Human Need to Feel Seen 74

Superstition as Emotional Shortcuts 81

Reflection Exercise: 87

Idioms Across Cultures 97

Why These Beliefs Survive 104

Three People, Same Sensation, Different Worlds 113

The Burn of the Digital Age 123

The Anxiety Loop 130

Rewriting the Story 138

Conclusion 146

WORKBOOK 153

DEFINED MODELS 159

A SHORT HISTORY OF BURNING EARS 162

AUTHOR'S NOTE 165

RECOMMENDED READING 167

GLOSSARY 173

REFERENCES 180

Preface

The Sensation That Starts the Story

My right ear heated up during a meeting that should have been dull. No pressure, no conflict, just routine work. The heat arrived without warning. It sharpened my focus and made me scan the room. I felt watched even though nobody looked my way. My body acted first. My thoughts scrambled to catch up.

That moment stayed with me because it felt unreasonable. I knew nobody was talking about me. I knew nothing had changed in the room. Yet my body reacted as if a social alarm had gone off. I left the meeting unsettled. I kept replaying it in my mind. The sensation stuck harder than the facts.

I recognised something important that day. Strange little sayings hold more truth than they seem to. When people ask, "Are your ears burning?", they anchor a superstition to a real human habit. We try to explain internal noise. We reach for patterns even when none exist. We treat our bodies as if they leak information about what others think of us.

I once felt a threat that never arrived. My ear heated up, my chest tightened and my thoughts sprinted ahead. I reacted to a danger that did not exist. That was a false story.

Another time, I felt a sensation that told a truth. My stomach tightened as I walked into a room during a tense family dispute. I sensed the mood shift before anyone spoke. My body caught the tone faster than my mind. That was a correct story.

Our bodies speak all the time. Our minds rush to answer. Sometimes we get it right. Often we get it wrong. This book explains why.

It follows a simple path:

- where the superstition came from
- how the body creates these sensations
- how the brain misreads them
- why culture keeps old stories alive
- how modern life triggers ancient instincts

You will see how folklore shaped early explanations, how biology produces noise, how psychology builds meaning and how culture pushes those meanings into your daily life. You will see why your body jumps in early and why your thoughts arrive late.

Researchers like Sapolsky, Kahneman and van der Kolk show that we live in conflict between instinct and logic. Their work helps frame the deeper point of this book ~ your sensations are signals, not prophecies.

If you want clarity instead of confusion, start by paying attention to the moment your body speaks before you do. That is where every story begins.

PART I

THE ROOT OF THE RUMOUR

Where the Saying Really Comes From

The idea that burning ears reveal hidden talk did not begin as a joke. It started with the Romans. They believed the body reacted to events that happened out of sight. They treated sensations as messages. They tracked flushes, twitches and sudden heat as signs of what other people said or thought. A burning ear belonged to a broader system they used to manage uncertainty.

Pliny the Elder recorded this belief clearly. He wrote that a person with heat in the right ear was being praised. A person with heat in the left ear was being criticised. This simple claim spread through Roman society. Nobody questioned it. The belief fit the culture. People saw their bodies as surfaces that reflected social and spiritual forces. Flesh acted like a public notice. Your skin revealed your reputation.

Romans interpreted many signs this way. A twitch under the left eye warned of trouble. A sharp pain in the thigh signalled conflict. A sudden shiver meant someone walked over the place where you would be buried. These claims lacked evidence, but they offered fast answers. People made sense of the unknown by linking internal signals to external events. They wanted control in a world filled with risk.

The belief moved through Europe as Roman influence shaped new regions. It survived the fall of the empire because it solved a daily need. People still wanted certainty. They still wanted explanations for sensations that arrived without warning. A burning ear gave them a quick story. Even if the story was wrong, it created comfort. A short saying provided direction during social tension.

Rural communities in early Europe depended on tight social circles. Reputation changed quickly. A rumour travelled through a village in an afternoon. People needed ways to manage what they could not see. A sudden heat in one ear helped them make decisions. They could stay alert, adjust their behaviour or prepare for a shift in mood. The belief acted like a tool for social navigation.

Written records from the Middle Ages show this pattern clearly. Chroniclers noted how villagers linked sensations to hidden events. A tingling palm meant money. A twitching eyelid meant a visitor. A burning ear meant people spoke about you. These notes appeared in sermons, diaries and letters. They helped people manage uncertainty long before modern science appeared.

As printing grew, early almanacs collected sayings, farming tips and local advice. Burning ears sat beside weather guides and planting charts. Readers treated all of it as common sense. When a superstition arrives bundled with practical information, it gains credibility. It feels like part of the natural order.

The saying reached English readers through these printed collections. Early versions varied slightly. Some kept the Roman distinction between right and left. Others simplified the idea into a single claim. The meaning stayed the same. A burning ear signalled someone was talking about you. This mix of variation and consistency kept the belief stable across generations.

As theatre and poetry grew, writers began using the phrase on stage. They placed it in dialogue to reveal suspicion or confidence. Audiences recognised the meaning without explanation. The line spread through public speech because it was short, flexible and familiar. People repeated it at home, adopted it into jokes and passed it to their children.

The belief survived major scientific advances. Medical explanations did not replace it. People accepted that blood flow and nerve activity could cause sudden heat, yet they still relied on older stories. Science described the mechanism, but it did not address the emotional punch. It did not explain why the sensation felt personal. Superstition filled that gap. It offered meaning instead of measurement.

A superstition lasts when it meets emotional needs. Researchers like Frazer and Radford show how these small beliefs stay alive. A short saying becomes part of a group identity. It moves easily through conversation. It eases awkward moments. It helps people explain confusing sensations. It also creates connection. People laugh when they say it. They tease each other. The phrase becomes social glue.

Dunbar's work adds another layer. Humans spend large parts of their mental life thinking about other people. We monitor relationships constantly. We track alliances and status. We watch for signs of acceptance or rejection. Romans acted this way. So did medieval villagers. So do you. The brain searches for clues about how others see you. A burning ear feels like one of those clues.

Picture a simple moment. Someone sits at a dinner table. The conversation moves around them. Their right ear heats up. They straighten their posture. They scan the room without turning their head. They feel watched even if nobody is looking. Their mind builds a story within seconds. That story arrives faster than reason. It shows how instinct drives interpretation.

The timing of sensation also matters. Body changes often occur during social situations. If your ear warms when you walk into a room, your mind links the two events. You assume a connection because the brain hates randomness. You want a story. You want clarity. Even if the heat came from stress, alcohol or temperature change, the mind still looks outward.

Language protected the superstition across centuries. Short sayings work like tools. They pass through generations because they stick to memory. Children hear them from adults. They repeat them without questioning them. They carry them into adulthood because the line feels familiar. Familiarity often wins over accuracy.

The phrase also survived because it never demanded full belief. People could take it lightly. You could repeat it even if you doubted it. You could use it as a joke or a hint. This flexibility helped the belief drift through time without friction. Rigid claims die when they fail. Flexible claims survive. Burning ears stayed flexible.

The historical path of this saying reveals a deeper truth. Humans struggle with unexplained internal noise. When a sudden sensation appears, the mind searches for a cause. Social explanations come first. The body reacts to stress, temperature or emotion, yet the mind pushes toward stories about other people. This pattern began long before science. It still shapes reactions today.

Think about a modern example. A person heads into a meeting. Their ear warms as they reach the doorway. The people inside stop talking as they enter. The timing forms a neat picture. They assume the group discussed them. The story feels right even if the silence had nothing to do with them. The sensation fills the gap. The mind follows.

This process shows how superstition becomes habit. It shows how an old Roman claim sits inside daily life without effort. It shows how a tiny sensation carries social weight. The belief persists because the sensation feels personal and the story feels satisfying.

You now have the full picture of how the saying formed, travelled and settled into modern speech. The next chapter shows how people once lived in a world where every sensation carried meaning. That world shaped the instincts that still influence you today.

2

When the Body Was an Omen

Before science, people lived in a world where every sensation carried meaning. A twitch, a shiver or a flush did not feel random. It felt like a sign. People believed their bodies acted as channels for unseen forces. They linked internal changes to moral, social or spiritual events. This habit formed across cultures because people needed explanations at a time when most causes remained hidden.

A burning cheek could mean someone spoke your name with anger. A ringing ear could signal gossip. A twitching eyelid could warn of a visitor. A sudden chill could predict misfortune. These beliefs made the world feel organised. They offered reasons for sensations that arrived without warning. They helped people prepare for events beyond their control.

Early communities relied heavily on these small cues. Life carried risk. Illness spread quickly. Travel was limited. Social standing shaped survival. People wanted signs that guided them. They needed fast ways to read intention or danger. Their bodies became the first place they searched for answers.

In villages across Europe, people watched their own sensations closely. They also watched the reactions of others. If someone clutched their chest or rubbed their ear, neighbours built stories around it. Sensations became public information. A person who felt a sudden heat might change their posture, tone or behaviour. Others noticed. The belief spread through observation as much as speech.

Writers from the Middle Ages recorded these habits. They noted how people used bodily signs as part of ordinary life. A tingling foot before a journey meant a smooth trip. A sudden itch on the scalp meant an argument nearby. A flush on one side of the face meant shame linked to a hidden action. These notes were not satire. They reflected common thought.

The system made sense within its own logic. People did not have machines or instruments to measure internal states. They relied on sensation as data. The body served as a warning device. A single sensation could shape a decision. It guided conversations, choices and movements. If an omen signalled trouble, people prepared themselves emotionally or spiritually.

This approach remained stable because it delivered emotional comfort. A sign stops uncertainty. It helps people act. Even if the sign is incorrect, it reduces fear. A burning ear offered a clean answer. Someone was speaking about you. The explanation removed doubt. It made the body feel connected to the social world. The feeling of connection was more important than accuracy.

A short example shows how powerful this habit was. Picture a woman in a small town in the fifteenth century. She works in a shared courtyard. Her left cheek heats suddenly. She stops. She glances at her neighbours. She assumes someone speaks poorly of her. She changes her behaviour for the rest of the day. She withdraws from conversation. She avoids a family she suspects. A small sensation shapes her social world. The belief guides her because she trusts it more than silence.

Magical thinking played a strong role. People wanted to believe the world sent them signals. They wanted support from something larger than themselves. A sensation felt like contact from a higher force. A warm ear hinted at moral judgement. A shiver hinted at danger. A twitch hinted at fortune. These interpretations spread because they comforted people who lived with fear and uncertainty.

This habit also protected people from helplessness. When a sensation struck, the belief gave them a sense of control. They felt prepared, even if nothing happened. The physical change provided a starting point. They moved from sensation to meaning. The belief helped them avoid confusion. Confusion felt unsafe. Meaning felt steady.

Over time, these ideas blended into early scientific thought. As scholars studied the body, they challenged older claims. They explained that heat, redness and tingling came from blood flow and nerves. They explained that shivers came from temperature changes. They explained that ringing ears came from pressure and sound sensitivity. The explanations improved, but the emotional habits stayed. People wanted stories, not just mechanisms.

This transition did not remove superstition. It reshaped it. People learned scientific descriptions while still holding older beliefs in the background. A person could understand circulation yet still tease a friend about burning ears. The shift created two layers of interpretation. One layer belonged to biology. The other layer belonged to emotion. People used both.

To understand why superstition lasted, consider a simple modern scene. A person waits for a text message after an argument. Their stomach tightens. They feel heat in their face. They assume the other person is speaking about them. They interpret the sensation as evidence of conflict. The logic matches the old pattern. Sensation first, story second. The instinct has not changed. Only the context has.

Frazer, Ariely and Radford highlight the same point in their work. People create meaning before they create accuracy. They want narrative more than proof. They seek structure more than certainty. Bodily omens delivered structure. They gave people a way to sort feelings into categories. They turned the unknown into something that looked understandable.

The key element is simplicity. Bodily omens thrived because they required no tools. Anyone could use them. Anyone could share them. People built community through shared interpretation. They taught their children which sensations meant fortune or danger. They repeated sayings during meals and rituals. These habits formed part of cultural identity.

The habit stayed because it aligned with human biology. Sensations arrive fast. Thoughts arrive slow. The mind wants fast explanation. The old beliefs answered that need. Even when they were wrong, they calmed the discomfort of uncertainty.

This chapter shows that ancient people did not act irrationally. They acted within their limits. They used the tools they had. They read their bodies because their bodies were the most accessible source of information. The instinct that drove them still drives you. You continue to link sensations to meaning even when you know the science. You do this because it feels natural.

The next chapter shows how this instinct plays out in real time. You will see how a person misreads a sudden sensation and builds a story around it. You will see how childhood experiences shape that story. You will see how the mind uses sensation as evidence even when nothing has happened. This pattern forms the core of the struggle between instinct and clarity.

3

Case Study:

The Woman Who Felt the Room Change

A woman named Sara worked in a small marketing firm. Her job involved regular meetings, shared projects and constant group discussion. She liked clear information and disliked sudden changes. She preferred predictable days. She also carried an old habit from childhood. She watched people closely. She tracked tone, posture and mood. She noticed small shifts that others missed.

One Monday morning, she sat at her desk sorting emails. The office felt calm. Most people typed quietly. A few held low conversations. She felt settled until she sensed heat rising in her right ear. The warmth grew sharp. It lifted her awareness. She sat still. She listened harder. She felt watched even though nobody looked at her.

Her mind responded before she chose a thought. She wondered who spoke about her. She assumed the heat meant she had become the subject of a private conversation. She scanned the room without moving her head. A group of colleagues stood near the printer. They were laughing softly. She linked the heat in her ear to their laughter. The link felt solid even though nothing supported it.

This reaction came from a pattern she developed early in life. When she was twelve, she watched her parents argue in the kitchen. She felt a rush of heat in her face before she heard any raised voices. She remembered that moment clearly. Her body reacted before the argument became audible. She learned to trust these sensations. She believed they protected her from conflict. She expected physical changes to signal danger.

In adulthood, the same instinct triggered during ordinary moments. The heat in her ear felt like a clue. She felt exposed. Her pulse rose. Her palms warmed. She held her breath for a second. She waited for a sign that confirmed her suspicion. She did not have evidence, but the sensation pushed her toward a story. She filled the gap with fear.

This habit formed the start of a loop. Sensation created meaning. Meaning shaped emotion. Emotion reinforced the story. The more she focused on the heat in her ear, the more significant it felt. The sensation grew as her attention intensified. She assumed this growth meant the story was correct. Her mind built a structure around a single physical change.

To understand her reaction, you need to see how her attention worked. She noticed the group near the printer. She noticed one person covering their mouth while laughing. She noticed a glance that may not have been directed at her. These cues did not carry clear meaning. She filled the gaps with her own assumptions. Her body felt threatened, so her mind searched for evidence. She found patterns because she needed them, not because they existed.

Sara stood to refill her water bottle. As she walked past the group, they stopped laughing. This pause had nothing to do with her. One colleague had been telling a story about a weekend mishap and paused to answer a question. The timing looked suspicious to Sara. She linked the pause to her presence. Her ear still felt warm. The heat became proof that she had been the topic.

Her thoughts built momentum. She replayed an interaction from the previous week. She had disagreed with a colleague about a project timeline. She now believed that disagreement triggered comments behind her back. She linked the heat in her ear to that memory. The logic felt convincing because the body sensation made the memory vivid.

This pattern illustrates a core principle from Kahneman. The mind creates quick stories that feel complete. It prefers fast coherence to slow analysis. A sensation speeds up this process. It gives the mind something to anchor to. The anchor becomes the centre of the story. Every detail circles it.

Damasio's work explains the biological side. A physical change becomes an emotional signal. The signal travels faster than thought. The body sets the frame. This frame guides interpretation. You feel first. You think second.

Sara returned to her desk. The warmth faded slowly, but the story stayed. The sensation had already shaped her emotions. She avoided eye contact with the group near the printer. She typed faster. She felt tense for the rest of the morning. Her behaviour changed even though nothing concrete had happened.

This case shows how easily a person can misread a signal. A small sensation becomes a clue. A guess becomes a belief. A belief shapes behaviour. Once the loop starts, each step reinforces the next. The story builds strength from repetition.

Another point matters here. Sara grew up in a home where she had to monitor tension to stay safe. Her family environment trained her nervous system to react quickly. She learned early that small cues hinted at real conflict. In her adult life, this habit resurfaced even when the cues carried no meaning. Her past shaped her present. Her childhood taught her to treat sensations as warnings.

Modern workplaces still trigger these old patterns. Open offices bring unpredictable noise, shifting conversations and uneven social signals. People see private talk, closed doors and sudden pauses. They link these moments to their own fears. A physical sensation amplifies the concern. The body becomes part of the social environment.

To understand how common this reaction is, consider a short comparison. Two people sit in the same office. Both feel a warm ear at different moments. One person ignores it. They assume it comes from temperature, stress or a quick rush of blood. They move on. The other person interprets it as a sign. They search for meaning. They read the room. They build a story. The difference lies not in the sensation but in the interpretation. Experience shapes the story. Sensitivity shapes the response.

Sara's case reveals the pattern that runs through this book. Sensation arrives. Meaning follows. Emotion locks it in. The body speaks first. The mind rushes to fill the silence with a narrative. This habit kept people safe thousands of years ago. It now creates confusion in ordinary modern settings.

You will see this pattern again. The next chapter shows the biology that produces these sensations. You will learn what actually causes the heat, the flush and the sudden spike of awareness. When you see the mechanism clearly, the story becomes easier to manage.

Jason A. Solomon, B.Ed

PART II

THE BIOLOGY OF THE BURN

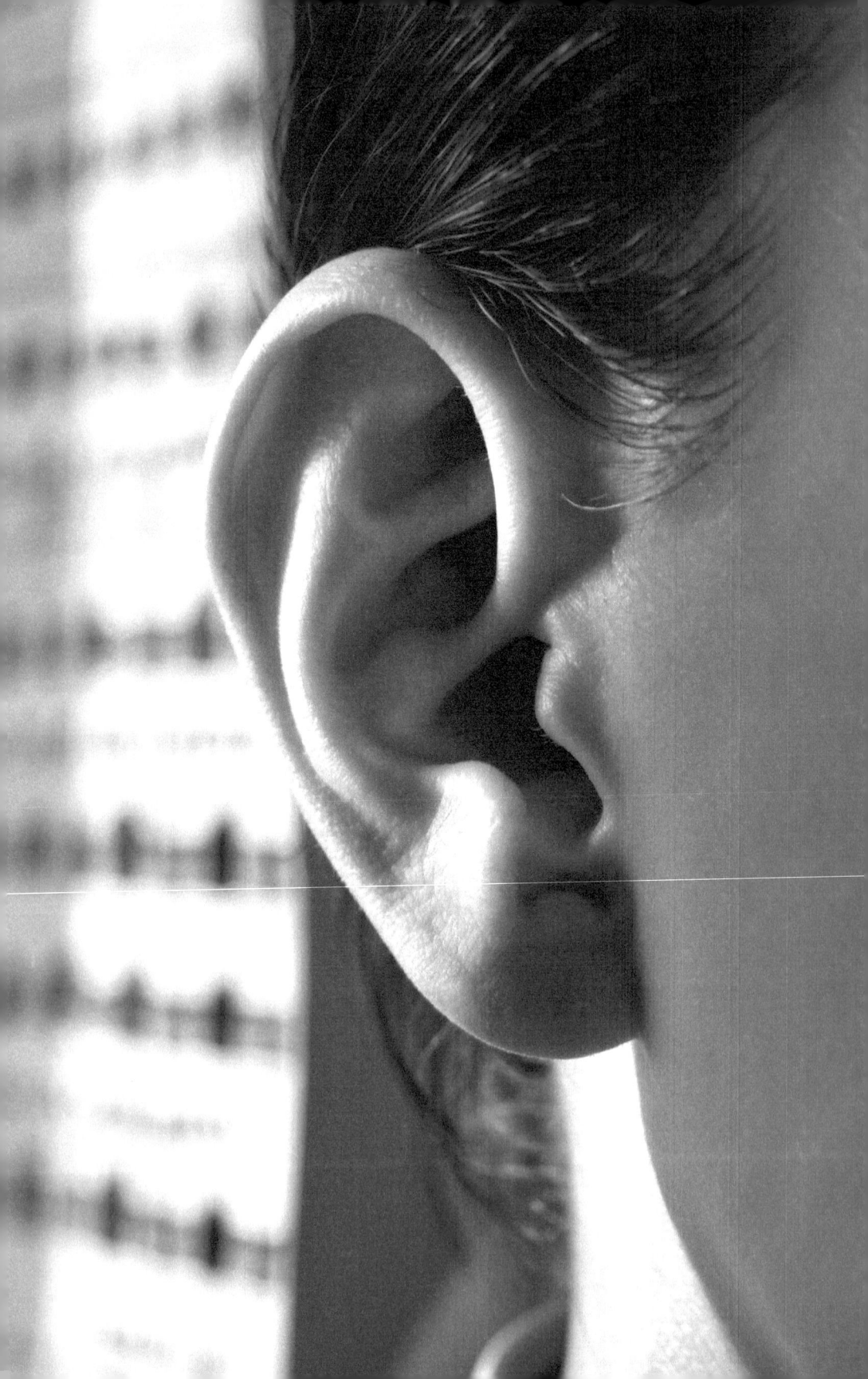

4

What a Burning Ear Actually Is

A burning ear feels personal because it strikes fast. The heat arrives without warning. It draws attention to itself. It makes you feel as if something meaningful is happening. The sensation stands out because it is sudden, visible and easy to notice. The truth is simple. A burning ear comes from changes in blood flow, nerve activity and temperature. The body creates the heat. The mind turns it into a message.

The skin on the ear is thin. Blood vessels sit close to the surface. When those vessels widen, warm blood moves through quickly. The heat rises. The colour changes. This widening is called vasodilation. It is an ordinary function of the body. It responds to temperature, emotion, hormones and stress.

One common trigger is embarrassment. When you feel judged, the body shifts blood to the skin on the face and neck. The ears sit inside that response. Anger creates a similar effect. Stress hormones push blood outward. The skin warms. The temperature rise feels sharp. You notice it because the ears do not have much padding. Heat travels through them faster than it travels through thicker areas of the body.

Cold weather also sets the stage. When you move from a cold space into a warm one, frozen blood vessels open quickly. The ears heat up as they adjust. The contrast makes the change feel stronger. People often mistake this reaction for a social cue because the sudden shift feels like it carries meaning.

Another trigger comes from rapid attention shifts. When your focus sharpens, your body prepares for action. Heart rate climbs. Blood flow increases. Your ears may heat as part of this small surge. You may notice it during meetings, conversations or moments when you expect judgement. The sensation becomes tied to social tension, even if the cause was biological.

Hormones also play a role. Small changes in cortisol, adrenaline or oestrogen create temperature shifts. These changes happen throughout the day. They rise and fall with sleep cycles, energy levels and stress patterns. Many of these shifts never reach awareness. When they do, they feel sudden because your attention was not on your body until the sensation stated itself.

Random nerve firing adds another layer. The nervous system sends signals that do not always match events. Sometimes a nerve misfires. Sometimes it reacts to pressure from a headset, hat or phone. Sometimes a tiny change in posture affects blood flow. These changes feel like heat or tingling. The brain notices them because they break the background noise of the body.

Interoception explains how you sense these signals. Interoception is your ability to detect internal states. Some people notice small changes quickly. Others barely detect anything at all. High interoceptive sensitivity means you feel your body clearly. This skill helps with emotional awareness but also increases the risk of misreading sensations. If you feel every shift, you may give each shift meaning.

Craig's research shows how interoception works inside the brain. Signals travel from the body through the spinal cord into areas that process emotion and attention. These signals reach the emotional centres before the logical centres. This timing means you feel something before you understand it. Critchley shows this same pattern in studies on awareness and anxiety. The body speaks faster than thought.

Van der Kolk's work shows how past experiences shape the strength of these signals. People with histories of stress, conflict or trauma often have stronger responses. Their nervous systems react quickly. A burning ear may feel louder to them. The sensation may feel more urgent because their body learned to treat internal changes as warnings.

To see how the mechanism works in daily life, picture two simple scenes. In the first, a man walks into a room after a brisk walk. His ears heat up because of the temperature shift and the increase in blood flow. He sits down near a group of colleagues. The heat fades within minutes. He does not think about it.

In the second scene, someone enters a room after an argument. Their body remains tense. Their heart rate stays high. Their ears heat up for the same biological reasons. But this person feels watched. Their mind links the heat to the conflict. The sensation becomes a clue. The biology did not change. Only the interpretation changed.

This difference matters. The body creates signals automatically. The meaning comes later. When you understand the mechanism, the sensation feels less mysterious. You see it as part of the body's normal function, not as proof that someone is talking about you.

Sensitivity also differs across people. Some have strong vascular responses. Others have subtle ones. Some feel heat quickly. Others rarely notice these shifts. Genetics, hormones, lifestyle and stress all shape these differences. There is no single standard. What feels intense for one person may feel minor for another.

The ear is a hotspot because of its structure. It has a high density of small blood vessels. It reacts fast to emotional states. It reacts fast to temperature. It reacts fast to stress. The speed of the change makes it noticeable. You feel the heat before you think about the cause. That timing shapes the story.

A burning ear also feels important because it is visible. People see redness on their own skin. They feel exposed. Visibility creates self focus. You assume others can see what you feel. You assume they read meaning into your reaction. This social pressure makes the sensation feel larger than it is.

Understanding the biology behind a burning ear does not reduce the intensity. It reduces the confusion. When you know the cause, you do not need to guess. You do not need to create stories that increase anxiety. You see the sensation as a neutral signal rather than a sign of judgement.

The body produces these signals constantly. You only notice a few. Your attention selects what stands out. Sudden heat stands out. Sudden tingling stands out. When you catch these changes, the brain tries to explain them. It builds a story that fits your fears or expectations. That story feels convincing because the sensation is real.

This chapter strips the mystery from the sensation. You know what creates the heat. You know how the signal travels. You know why some people notice it more than others. The next chapter explains why your brain dislikes unexplained sensations and why it tries to create patterns even when nothing meaningful happened.

5

The Brain Hates Randomness

Your body produces noise all day. It sends heat, tingles, pulses, pressure shifts and changes in rhythm. Most of this noise never reaches awareness. The moments that do reach awareness feel personal. Sudden sensations draw your focus. When you cannot explain the signal, the brain reacts. It wants order. It wants a clean story that removes uncertainty. It dislikes gaps. It fills those gaps before you even notice the process.

Pattern recognition sits at the centre of this response. Humans evolved to detect threat early. The brain scans for patterns that support survival. It looks for repeated shapes, sounds, movements and cues. It also looks for patterns inside the body. A burning ear becomes part of this system. It stands out from the baseline. The brain reacts by searching for a cause.

When you feel something strange, the mind builds a quick explanation. Kahneman calls this fast thinking. It produces stories at high speed. These stories feel complete even when they are based on limited information. The brain does not want accuracy first. It wants certainty. Certainty reduces stress. A story, even a wrong one, feels safer than confusion.

This instinct explains why a burning ear often triggers social interpretation. Social life shaped survival. Early humans needed to know who liked them, who disliked them and who posed a threat. The mind learned to link social cues with bodily reactions. When a sensation appears without an obvious cause, the mind leans toward social explanation.

Consider a simple moment. A man sits on a bus. His ear heats suddenly. His brain notices the change. It searches for a pattern. He recalls two people behind him talking softly. He links the heat to them. He assumes they spoke about him even though he cannot hear their words. The sensation came from blood flow. The story came from pattern detection.

Availability bias also shapes this process. Your brain pulls the most recent or emotional memory to explain a new sensation. If you argued with someone yesterday, a burning ear today feels connected. If you felt judged in a meeting last week, the heat feels linked to that moment. The brain retrieves the most accessible explanation. It rarely checks if the explanation fits.

Another bias is the illusion of causality. Humans often believe that two events occurring near each other must be linked. Sensation plus social cue equals meaning. You enter a room and feel a warm ear. People pause their conversation. You assume they paused because of you. The timing creates the illusion of connection. The brain accepts the illusion because it removes uncertainty.

This habit becomes stronger when you feel anxious. Anxiety narrows your focus. It pushes your attention toward threat. Small cues become significant. A slight movement, a lowered voice or a casual glance feels loaded. The sensation in your ear becomes a spotlight that intensifies those cues. Anxiety turns coincidence into evidence.

A short example shows how this works. A woman walks into a cafeteria. She feels heat on one side of her face. She sees two people look in her direction. They look away quickly. She assumes the heat and the glances are linked. The story forms in seconds. She feels exposed. The reality is simple. The glances were random. The heat came from her walk up the stairs. The link exists only inside her mind.

Sapolsky's work shows that the brain values prediction. When events feel predictable, stress decreases. When events feel random, stress rises. A burning ear feels random. The brain tries to predict its meaning. The fastest prediction is social attention. This prediction reduces the discomfort of randomness. It gives you a sense of control.

People often underestimate how much the brain guesses. Guessing is automatic. The brain does not notify you when it fills gaps. It produces a story that feels seamless. You rarely see the guess forming. You only feel the result. The result feels true because the body signal reinforces it. The connection appears strong. In reality, the connection comes from speed, not evidence.

Pattern recognition helps explain why superstitions persist. Superstitions offer simple rules for noisy situations. When a sensation appears, a superstition supplies an immediate answer. It removes the burden of analysis. It satisfies the brain's dislike of uncertainty. The brain rewards this satisfaction. It repeats the superstition the next time the sensation appears.

Another factor is confirmation bias. Once you believe a sensation means something, you notice moments that support the belief. You ignore moments that contradict it. If you think burning ears mean someone is talking about you, you will remember the times you felt heat and later heard someone mention your name. You will forget the many times you felt the heat and nothing happened. The belief grows even when the evidence remains inconsistent.

This bias shapes social interpretation as well. If you worry about how others see you, you will connect sensations to that fear. You will notice any cue that fits your concern. You will skip cues that show you are safe. The sensation becomes a trigger. It activates old patterns that feel convincing even when they are not accurate.

To see how strong these biases can be, look at a brief scenario. A team sits in a meeting room. One person feels heat in their ear while speaking. They assume a colleague disagrees with them. They notice a slight head tilt. They interpret it as disapproval. The meaning becomes clear inside their mind. After the meeting, they avoid the colleague. The colleague, unaware of this, wonders why the relationship changed. The shift started with a misread sensation.

The brain also struggles with randomness in internal states. When you feel a sudden change inside your body, the lack of context creates tension. The tension demands explanation. The fastest explanation often comes from social life. If the environment contains any ambiguous cue, the mind seizes it. Ambiguous cues invite interpretation. You fill the gaps with fear, memory or expectation.

This instinct makes sense biologically. The cost of missing a threat once outweighed the cost of overreacting many times. The brain leans toward caution. It would rather create a false connection than ignore a potential danger. This survival habit still shapes reactions today, even when the real risk is low.

The brain dislikes randomness because randomness feels unsafe. A burning ear stands out because it is unpredictable. Your mind wants to solve it quickly. That fast solution becomes a story. The story lingers long after the sensation fades.

Understanding this process helps you break it. When you recognise that your brain builds stories based on speed, not evidence, you gain distance. You learn to question the first explanation that appears. You learn to separate sensation from meaning.

This chapter shows why your mind creates stories from small signals. The next chapter gives you tools. You will learn how to test these patterns in your own body. You will see how attention changes sensation. You will see how expectation creates physical reactions. These experiments give you insight into your own interoception and reveal how easily the mind bends sensation into narrative.

6

Experiments You Can Try

Your body delivers thousands of signals each day. Most pass unnoticed. A few break through. The ones you notice feel important because they interrupt your attention. These experiments help you see what actually drives those sensations. They give you a clearer picture of how your body behaves and how your mind interprets small changes. When you understand the process, you stop treating every signal as a message.

You do not need specialised equipment. You only need time, awareness and a quiet space. Take each experiment slowly. Do not push past your limits. The goal is clarity, not intensity.

INTEROCEPTION AWARENESS TEST

Interoception describes your ability to sense internal states. Some people detect small shifts quickly. Others detect only strong sensations. This test shows where you sit on that scale.

Sit upright with both feet on the floor. Set a timer for one minute. Close your eyes. Place one hand on your chest. Focus on the heartbeat inside your body. Count the beats you feel. Do not touch your pulse. When the minute ends, take your actual pulse for fifteen seconds. Multiply the number by four. Compare the two numbers.

If your numbers match closely, you have strong interoception. You feel small changes inside your body. If the numbers differ widely, you rely more on external cues. Neither pattern is better. Both come with strengths and risks. Strong interoception helps you recognise stress early, but it can also make neutral sensations feel significant. Low interoception protects you from sensory overload, but it can make it harder to detect early signs of emotional strain.

Repeat the test in different states. Try it after exercise, after a stressful moment, after rest and before sleep. You will see how context changes your awareness.

THE ATTENTION AMPLIFIER

This experiment reveals how attention increases sensation. People often assume sensations appear on their own. In truth, attention shapes intensity.

Sit still and choose a neutral area of the body. Your left ear works well. Do not touch it. Watch it with your mind. Search for sensation. Within moments, most people feel warmth, tingling or a shift in pressure. These sensations result from blood flow, temperature and small changes in muscle tension. They feel strong because attention magnifies them.

Now switch attention suddenly to the right ear. You may feel a different pattern. The difference comes from attention, not meaning.

This experiment shows why burning ears feel urgent. Once you notice heat, you monitor it. Monitoring intensifies the sensation.

THE SUGGESTION TEST

Suggestion shapes perception. When you expect sensation, your body cooperates. This test shows how quickly expectation changes physical responses.

Tell yourself you will feel heat in the right ear within one minute. Sit quietly. Watch your body. Most people feel warmth rise, even faintly. This shift comes from attention, not social meaning.

Repeat with the left ear. Again, you will likely feel heat. The body responds to focus. The mind responds to expectation. This combination creates sensations that feel significant.

This explains why anxious people misinterpret signals. Expectation sets the stage. Anxiety fills the gaps.

THE MEMORY RESPONSE TEST

Memory triggers physical change. Your body reacts to recalled emotion as if the event is happening now. This experiment shows the strength of that link.

Sit comfortably. Think of a mild social embarrassment. Something safe. Hold the memory for thirty seconds. Watch your body. You may feel heat in your ears, pressure in your chest or tension across your shoulders. These shifts come from hormonal reactions triggered by the memory.

Clear your mind. Now recall a moment of praise or acceptance. Hold it for thirty seconds. Notice the shift. You may feel warmth again, but the warmth carries a different emotional shape. This difference shows how emotion changes interpretation.

Your body can produce the same sensation under fear and under approval. The difference sits in the story.

THE TEMPERATURE CONTRAST DEMONSTRATION

This demonstration shows how ears heat quickly under basic physiological conditions.

Apply a cold cloth to your right ear for thirty seconds. Remove it. Wait a few seconds. You will feel warmth rise. The heat feels sharp. It has no social meaning. It comes from blood vessels opening after being constricted.

Repeat with the left ear. You will see small differences in timing and intensity. These differences show how variable signals can be.

Once you see how easy it is to trigger heat, you stop treating it as evidence of attention from others.

THE ANTICIPATION–REACTION LOOP

This exercise shows the loop between sensation and thought.

Sit quietly. Focus on your left ear. Tell yourself you will feel heat in thirty seconds. When the heat arrives, note your next thought. Many people jump straight to interpretation. They seek reasons. They search memories. They read the room.

Now reverse the order. Think of a social situation that worries you. Imagine being observed. Watch your body. Sensations appear quickly. You may feel the very signal you feared.

This loop shows why the mind misinterprets the body. Sensation and thought influence each other until you cannot tell which came first.

THE FALSE SIGNAL TEST

This test reveals how easily you can misinterpret a sensation when placed in a social frame. Sit in a room with low background noise. Focus on your right ear. Wait for even the smallest shift in temperature or tingling. Now pair the sensation with a thought such as, "Someone is talking about me right now." Hold that thought for fifteen seconds. Notice how fast the thought feels believable. The sensation gives the thought weight.

Now repeat the cycle with a neutral context. Tell yourself the same sensation means nothing. Watch how quickly the threat drains from your mind.

You learn two key points. Sensation feels real. Meaning does not.

THE POSTURE SHIFT TEST

Posture affects blood flow. Small changes create sensations that feel significant.

Sit upright for one minute. Then lean slightly to your left. Hold the position for twenty seconds. Return to centre. Notice your left ear. Many people feel a rise in warmth. The heat comes from altered circulation. It has no social meaning.

Repeat to the right side. Notice the difference. This simple test shows how easily neutral movements create signals that feel loaded.

THE NOISE–SIGNAL DISTINCTION EXERCISE

This exercise helps you sort neutral signals from meaningful ones.

Choose a sensation you notice often. It could be ear heat, a chest flutter or a small pulse in the neck. When the sensation appears, pause. Ask two questions.

- What happened in the thirty seconds before the sensation?
- What happened in the thirty seconds after?

If the answer is nothing, the sensation belongs to noise. You only treat it as meaningful when your mind makes a quick link. This exercise teaches you to delay interpretation. Delay reduces false stories.

WHY THESE EXPERIMENTS MATTER

These experiments reveal the same pattern again and again. Sensation comes first. Interpretation comes second. When you see how easily sensation shifts, you stop assuming the shift carries meaning. You understand the machinery behind it. You see how attention, memory, expectation and posture shape your internal world.

Damasio explains that the body sends signals to emotional centres before logical centres. This timing creates urgency. Craig shows how interoception makes some people feel these signals strongly. Critchley shows the link between anxiety and sensation. Their work supports what these exercises demonstrate. Your body behaves automatically. Your mind tries to explain it.

These exercises help you step out of that loop. When you see sensation clearly, you reduce the need for fast stories. You gain distance. You choose interpretation instead of reacting to it.

The next chapter explains why humans care so much about being talked about. You will see how the social brain shapes these reactions and why the body becomes a messenger in situations that do not require defence.

Jason A. Solomon, B.Ed

PART III

THE SOCIAL BRAIN AND INVISIBLE CONVERSATIONS

7

Why Humans Fear Being Talked About

Humans care about being judged because belonging once decided who survived and who did not. Early humans depended on cooperation to find food, protect children and defend against danger. A group offered safety. Being pushed out of that group placed someone at real risk. The nervous system learned this rule long before language formed. Your body still follows it. You react to social threat with the same circuits that once protected your ancestors from physical danger. This old wiring explains why even a small suspicion of being talked about can feel serious.

Reputation functioned as a basic survival tool. People watched how others behaved. Praise signalled trust. Criticism signalled weakness or conflict. Groups tolerated helpful members and removed those who placed others at risk. This constant scanning shaped the social brain. Dunbar's work shows that humans developed strong skills for reading tone, posture and small cues because these signals helped them navigate complex social structures. You inherited this ability. You look for signs of acceptance and rejection without thinking.

Gossip played a central role in keeping groups stable. It spread information quickly. People shared warnings about harmful behaviour and updates about cooperation. Gossip acted as a monitoring system long before laws or written rules existed. It helped the group identify who could be trusted. Even today, gossip still feels important because your brain interprets it as part of a threat detection system. A negative comment touches the same pathways involved in physical alarm. Your body reacts first. Your thoughts try to explain the reaction.

Fear of exclusion remains strong because humans still depend on acceptance. You want connection in workplaces, friendships and families. You want safety and respect. When you sense judgement, you fear losing these things. The fear shapes your interpretation of neutral cues. A slight pause in a conversation feels sharp. A look shared between people feels pointed. A burning ear feels suspicious even though the cause is biological.

Negative talk carries more weight than praise because it suggests risk. Praise supports identity, but it does not activate the survival system. Criticism threatens status. Your body reacts quickly when it senses a threat to identity because identity sits at the centre of social survival. Aronson's work on self-concept explains this clearly. Criticism feels dangerous because it hints at exclusion. Praise feels pleasant, but it rarely feels urgent.

This instinct forms early. Children watch adults to understand the world. They read tone and body language long before they understand sentences. A child who hears two adults whisper will feel tension even if the whisper has nothing to do with them. Their body picks up the shift before their mind can explain it. The same pattern appears on playgrounds. A child hears classmates laugh and feels heat rise in their cheeks. They assume the laughter is about them because their brain treats laughter without context as a signal of risk. Children carry these reactions into adolescence.

Teenagers experience the strongest version of this instinct. Their social world grows fast and unpredictable. Friend groups shift quickly. They receive constant feedback about appearance, status and behaviour. A whisper in a hallway or a delayed message online can feel like rejection. A teenager who walks into a classroom and sees two students glance their way will feel their chest tighten. Their ears heat. They assume the whisper is about them. Their body responds to social cues within seconds. Their thoughts follow. Online interactions strengthen this sensitivity. Missed messages, edited photos and vague comments create ongoing uncertainty. The teenager's body reacts before anything is confirmed.

Young adults carry this instinct into early careers and relationships. They want stability and respect. They need support from colleagues and partners. A person in their twenties may enter an office and see two colleagues pause at a screen. Their right ear warms. They assume the pause relates to them. They replay recent conversations, searching for mistakes or tension. Dating creates the same pattern. After a first date or a difficult discussion, a person may feel a sudden heat in their ear. Their mind links the heat to fear of rejection. The sensation becomes evidence for a story that does not exist.

Adults in their thirties and forties face structured environments where reputation still matters. Workplaces rely on cooperation. Gossip influences promotions and trust. A parent at a school event may see two teachers pause as they approach. Their ears warm. They assume the silence relates to them. They build a narrative about judgement based on a brief moment. The same instinct appears in family settings. A sibling's expression or a pause at the dinner table can trigger a physical reaction. The biology remains unchanged. The context shifts.

Older adults feel the instinct in different ways. People in later life care about relevance, dignity and respect. They want to maintain their place in families, workplaces and communities. A person in their sixties at a community event may notice two younger attendees exchange a glance. Their ear heats. They assume the glance relates to them. Their interpretation forms from decades of monitoring social cues. The instinct does not fade with age. It adapts to changing roles and expectations.

Across these stages, the pattern remains steady. You feel heat, tension or pressure. You search for meaning. You assume the meaning relates to your social standing. This happens because your brain treats social threat as a survival issue. Your ancestors relied on this system. You still carry it, even though the environment has changed.

The link between sensation and interpretation grows stronger when you worry about identity. People build their sense of self through feedback from others. You learn who you are by watching how people respond to you. When you feel watched or judged, identity feels unstable. You react strongly. You look for confirmation. A burning ear becomes part of that search. You assume the sensation reflects other people's thoughts.

The mind exaggerates these signals because small cues once held meaning. Humans evolved to react quickly to threat. A quiet conversation or a soft glance could once suggest danger. Today, these cues appear in ordinary situations. Your body does not know the difference. It responds to possibility, not evidence. You feel exposed even when nothing happened.

Modern life strengthens this instinct. Social media increases comparison. People receive feedback from large audiences. They see curated images, sharp comments and public reactions. They judge themselves more often. This habit spills into daily life. People become alert to how others see them. A burning ear feels like evidence of online scrutiny echoing into real conversations. The body repeats old instincts in new environments.

Personal history also shapes these reactions. People who grew up in unpredictable households learned to monitor others closely. They expect conflict. Their bodies react quickly to small shifts in tone or posture. They treat sensations as warnings. Someone with this background will misread a burning ear as danger because past experiences taught them to pay attention to small signals. Attachment patterns reinforce this. People with anxious attachment styles fear losing connection. They watch for signs of disapproval. A mild sensation becomes part of a wider story about rejection.

These reactions appear in countless daily scenes. A nine-year-old misreads a giggle. A teenager misreads a whisper. A twenty-three-year-old misreads a pause in an office. A forty-year-old misreads a glance at a school meeting. A sixty-eight-year-old misreads a murmur in a community group. The ages shift. The instinct stays steady. The body delivers the same signals it delivered to early humans who faced real danger from exclusion.

When you understand this pattern, you gain distance from it. You learn to question the link between sensation and meaning. You see how your body follows rules that no longer match the environment. You recognise that a burning ear reflects blood flow, not hidden talk. You stop assuming that every warm ear signals judgement.

This understanding becomes useful when sensations strike without warning. You can pause instead of rushing to a story. You can check the environment instead of trusting the first interpretation. You can separate biology from fear. The instinct still exists, but you learn how to live with it.

The next chapter explains how the social alarm system inside the brain creates fast reactions from tiny cues and why these cues trigger physical responses even when nobody is paying attention to you.

8

The Social Alarm System

Humans react to social cues faster than they react to deliberate thought. A small shift in someone's tone or posture can set off a chain of physical changes before you register what happened. These changes run on fast circuits inside the brain. They formed early in human history. You do not choose them. They occur because your biology prepares you for risk. The body responds first. The mind creates a story second. This sequence sits at the centre of what Sapolsky describes as automatic threat processing in social settings.

The system began with survival. Early humans lived in groups because isolation carried real danger. People relied on shared protection and resources. Anyone pushed out of the group faced harm. This pressure shaped the nervous system. It tuned the body to watch for signs of conflict or exclusion. A small change in tone or expression could mean trouble. Those who reacted early survived. Their traits passed forward. Dunbar's research on social group size supports this idea. He shows that humans evolved strong skills for reading tone, posture and small social signals.

These reactions start in the limbic system. This part of the brain responds to threat long before logical thought. It receives sensory input and acts in fractions of a second. It can trigger a flush in your ears, strain across your shoulders or changes in your breathing. These reactions form before the logical parts of the brain understand what happened. This timing matches what Kahneman describes as fast, automatic processing driven by instinct.

Humans behave as social scanners. You monitor faces, voices and small shifts in behaviour constantly. You do this even when you think you are relaxed. You check for tension in others. You listen for changes in tone. You watch for signs of approval or rejection. This constant scanning reflects the same mechanisms described by de Becker when he explains early threat recognition. Your biology checks for risk without your permission.

Mirror systems inside the brain strengthen this pattern. Humans copy the emotional states of people around them. Craig's work on interoception supports this idea. He shows how the brain blends internal sensation with the behaviour of others. If someone near you shows discomfort, you feel tension. If someone looks uneasy, your own body reacts. This supports cooperation, but it also produces false alarms. You feel sensations that are not yours. You assume the sensations relate to you.

This pattern intensifies in environments where reputation shapes outcomes. Schools, workplaces and community groups depend on cooperation. People care about how they appear. When you sense that someone may judge you, the social alarm system activates. It reacts fast because judgement once meant exclusion. A whisper or a short silence feels sharper than it is. Aronson's work on self concept explains why criticism feels heavier than praise. Criticism signals danger. Praise does not.

The brain dislikes uncertainty. It fills gaps with fast explanations. Kahneman describes this tendency as a shortcut used for speed, not accuracy. When the brain sees a glance or a shift in tone, it tries to explain it quickly. This creates errors. You assume people are reacting to you when they are not. The sensation arrives first. The story arrives second. The story feels convincing because your body already entered a state of alert.

People with unpredictable childhoods often carry a stronger version of this pattern. Van der Kolk explains how early instability shapes the nervous system. Children raised in unstable settings learn to read adults closely. They monitor tone and posture. They become sensitive to small shifts because these shifts matter. As adults, they respond quickly to uncertain cues. A pause in a conversation triggers tension. A quiet whisper creates heat in the ears. They treat these sensations as warnings.

Attachment history increases the intensity. Adults with anxious attachment expect rejection. They monitor cues that hint at loss. Their bodies respond quickly because their history trained them to react early. They assume sensations reflect judgement even when nothing happened.

Modern social environments intensify all of this. Social media removes tone and expression. People read messages without context. They see delayed replies and assume disinterest. They watch others online and feel pressure to match them. Turkle's work on digital behaviour highlights how constant online exposure creates ongoing social tension. Silence online becomes a signal of rejection. The alarm system fires more often because the brain sees many situations as uncertain.

A simple example shows this clearly. You walk into a meeting room. Two colleagues pause their discussion. Your left ear warms. Your stomach tightens. You assume they were talking about you. The reaction formed before you had time to analyse it. The alarm system detected a shift and prepared your body. Your mind created a story to match the sensation. Ariely explains how easily the mind redirects physical cues into meaning when uncertainty is high.

These reactions influence behaviour. People withdraw from groups because the sensations feel heavy. They misread pauses and silence as negative judgement. They react defensively to harmless comments. They form habits shaped by tension, not evidence.

Humans also misinterpret silence. Silence creates uncertainty. The brain treats uncertainty as risk. The alarm system activates. You feel discomfort and assume the discomfort reflects hidden information. The sensation becomes the evidence for the story.

Older adults carry the same automatic reactions. Their concerns change, but the underlying machinery stays. They still want respect and connection. They still monitor tone and posture. When they sense a shift, their bodies react. Their ears heat. Their chest tightens. The biology remains active.

Understanding this system gives you more control. When you feel a sudden physical reaction, you can pause. You can recognise that the sensation formed before the thought. You can ask whether anything real triggered it. Most of the time, nothing did. The reaction came from the body's habit of preparing for social risk. Sapolsky describes this as a mismatch between ancient biology and modern environments.

You can train yourself to wait for the logical parts of the brain. You can test the scene. You can look for evidence. You can recognise when the reaction belongs to the past rather than the present. You learn that sensation does not equal truth. You learn that heat or tension does not confirm anything about other people's thoughts.

When you see this clearly, the social alarm system loses its grip. You still feel the sensations, but you no longer treat them as messages. You understand the sequence. Sensation first. Story second. Biology decides the first half. You control the second.

The next chapter explores why humans sometimes feel mentioned even when nobody is speaking about them. It explains how the mind builds meaning from small cues and why intuition becomes unreliable in social settings shaped by uncertainty.

9

The Illusion of Feeling Mentioned

Humans detect social cues with remarkable speed. You notice tone, posture, direction of gaze and subtle changes in someone's voice before you form a clear thought. These signals reach your emotional centres early. Your brain reacts first. Your conscious mind arrives late. This lag creates confusion. You feel tension, heat or subtle pressure in your body and search for a cause. When the environment feels uncertain, the mind fills the space with an explanation. One common explanation is simple. Someone must be talking about you.

The illusion forms from several parts of human psychology. You carry an instinct to detect threat. You want to understand how people see you. You want to know where you stand. You treat silence, glances and whispers as possible signs of judgement. These reactions form from the same machinery explained by Kahneman. He describes how fast processing creates strong impressions long before careful reasoning begins. The fast system builds stories even when the details are thin.

When you sense small cues, your brain searches your environment for meaning. Low voices behind you signal something. Two people glancing at each other signal something. A sudden quiet in a group signals something. The sensation in your body reinforces this search. If your ear warms or your chest tightens at the same moment, you treat the sensation as evidence. You do not recognise that the sensation came from internal processes, not external actions. This confusion forms the illusion that you have been mentioned.

This illusion is common across cultures. Humans are social animals. They evaluate their standing constantly. They try to maintain connection and avoid exclusion. Aronson's research into self concept shows how sensitive humans are to any hint of judgement. When people feel insecure, they anchor their interpretations to the smallest cues. They would rather assume meaning than accept uncertainty. The brain dislikes gaps in explanation. It fills gaps with the quickest available story.

Small cues activate several systems at once. First, the sensory system detects a shift. Then the limbic system prepares your body for risk. Your interoceptive system delivers sensations. Your cognitive system tries to explain them. The process happens in seconds. The illusion appears because all these systems react at once and feed into each other. You feel something and assume the feeling reflects the environment.

You may walk into a room and feel heat rise in your ear. At the same time, a group stops speaking. The logical explanation might be that someone finished a sentence. The ancient explanation feels stronger. You assume you interrupted a conversation about you. The sensation makes the story feel right. The story makes the sensation feel personal. Craig's work on interoception explains this clearly. He shows how the brain merges body sensation with interpretation in a single process. You cannot separate them easily. The illusion feels real because your brain builds it from both sides.

People often attribute meaning to glances. A glance feels loaded when you feel insecure. You assume the glance reflects your behaviour or your appearance. You might think someone raised an eyebrow at you. In truth, they shifted their focus for an unrelated reason. Humans misinterpret neutral cues because they expect relevance. The social brain evolved to assume that other people's behaviour carries meaning. Dunbar highlights this in his research on social networks. He explains that humans survived by paying close attention to the actions of others.

Tone also creates confusion. You hear someone say something quietly and assume you caused the shift. You anchor your interpretation to the warm sensation in your body. You decide that the comment relates to you. This assumption rarely reflects reality. It reflects a mismatch between ancient instincts and modern interactions.

Projection plays a role. You project your fears onto the environment. If you fear criticism, you assume criticism has formed. If you fear exclusion, you assume exclusion has already begun. The body supports this assumption by producing signals that match the story. A burning ear, a rising pulse or a sense of pressure becomes part of the narrative. Ariely's work on decision making shows how people trust internal experiences even when the experiences contain errors.

People also misread whispers. Whispering feels secretive. Humans evolved to notice secrecy. Secrecy often signalled danger in early societies. Today, whispering may reflect a private discussion that has nothing to do with you. The alarm system still reacts. You feel tension. You feel heat. You assume the whisper belongs to your story. You forget that the brain responds to the possibility of threat, not the evidence of it.

Another factor strengthens the illusion. People see small patterns that do not exist. When you feel uncertain, your mind tries to link unrelated events. Kahneman explains this as the desire for coherence. Humans want their experiences to form a consistent picture. When you feel a sensation and see a cue at the same time, the brain treats them as connected. You forget that the timing was an accident. You misread coincidence as intention.

Insecurity fuels this process. When people feel stable, they interpret cues calmly. When they feel uncertain, they treat every sensation as meaningful. A tired parent hears two other parents speak quietly at a school event. Their ear warms. Their stomach tightens. They assume the whisper relates to their behaviour or their child. Their body delivered a stress response. Their mind filled the gap with a story shaped by fear.

Memory also influences the illusion. Past experiences shape interpretation. If you have been criticised before, you expect it again. If you grew up in an environment where people whispered about you, you anticipate similar events. Van der Kolk explains how memory shapes bodily reactions. The body reacts strongly when past experiences resemble the present situation. A similar cue triggers an old response. The sensation becomes stronger. The story feels familiar.

People with anxious attachment patterns experience this illusion more often. They worry about being ignored or replaced. They interpret cues through this fear. When their body reacts, they treat the reaction as confirmation. A slight rise in heat feels like evidence. A neutral glance feels like rejection. Their interpretation follows the same pattern seen in children who expect inconsistent attention.

Parasocial thinking adds another layer. Humans treat vague cues as personal even when they are not. You hear someone laugh behind you and assume the laugh relates to you. You see two people look in your direction and assume they judged your behaviour. De Becker highlights how people misread ordinary behaviour as threat when they lack information. The brain works hard to fill blanks. When information is missing, the mind creates meaning.

Anxiety increases these errors. Anxiety heightens attention to possible threats. It increases the intensity of body sensations. It shortens the time between sensation and interpretation. Critchley's work on anxiety and interoception shows that anxious people often misread internal signals. They feel sensations more strongly and treat them as meaningful. A warm ear feels like a social signal even though it came from blood flow or temperature.

This illusion appears across many settings. A teenager sits in a school corridor. Two classmates laugh at a joke unrelated to them. The teenager's ears heat. They assume the joke relates to their appearance. They feel embarrassed. Their chest tightens. They avoid eye contact because they believe they triggered the laugh.

A young adult begins a new role at work. They feel pressure to perform. They enter the lunch area and see two colleagues speak quietly. Their ear warms. They assume the conversation involves them. They replay their actions from earlier that morning. They feel unsettled. They misread the glance as judgement.

A parent arrives at a community event. A group stops speaking because they reached the end of a discussion. The parent's body reacts. Their ear warms. They assume the conversation involved their child. They feel slight panic. They worry about reputation. They forget that conversations naturally rise and fall.

An older adult hears whispering at a social gathering. Their ear heats slightly. Their mind links the sensation to the whisper. They believe someone judged their behaviour or clothing. They withdraw from the group. They misinterpret the situation because their body reacted to uncertainty.

These examples show the same sequence. Sensation. Interpretation. Projection. None reflect the truth. The illusion forms because the brain wants to protect you. It reacts to uncertainty. It avoids risk by assuming meaning. This instinct once kept people safe. Today it misfires.

Humans also struggle with ambiguous cues. Ambiguous cues allow many interpretations. A quiet tone could reflect fatigue. A glance could reflect distraction. A whisper could reflect a topic unrelated to you. The alarm system dislikes ambiguity. It wants clarity. It responds with physical sensation. Your body anchors the interpretation. You assume the meaning relates to you because the sensation feels personal.

The illusion grows stronger when multiple cues appear at once. Heat in your ear plus a whisper feels more significant than either cue alone. You assume the combination reflects intention. You forget that internal and external cues do not sync intentionally. They sync by chance. Kahneman describes this pattern as the mind's preference for simple explanations. The mind connects dots that do not belong together because connection feels safer than uncertainty.

Your identity influences the illusion. People want to feel seen. They want relevance. They want to matter. Even negative attention can feel meaningful. Humans want to play a role in the group. When uncertainty rises, they interpret sensation as a sign that others are thinking about them. This satisfies the mind's desire for relevance. Dunbar explains how group belonging remains one of the strongest drivers of human behaviour.

People sometimes feel mentioned because they want to understand how others see them. They want clarity. They want a stable sense of self. When they cannot access that clarity directly, they rely on sensation. They treat sensation as information. They forget that sensation comes from physiology, not social feedback.

The illusion becomes stronger during stress. Stress sharpens the social alarm system. It increases attention to small cues. It increases the intensity of body reactions. Sapolsky explains how stress prepares the body for threat even when no threat exists. A person under stress treats sensations as warnings. They assume negative intention. They build stories from incomplete information.

Once the illusion forms, it reinforces itself. You feel sensation. You assume meaning. You believe the meaning. You feel more sensation. The body responds to the story you created. This cycle feels coherent. It feels convincing. You forget that it began with a single neutral cue.

Breaking the illusion requires awareness. You need to notice the sequence. Sensation first. Story second. The mind does not create the sensation. The body does. You can pause. You can check the scene. You can ask whether anything real happened. Most of the time, nothing occurred. The reaction came from physiology.

You can also test your assumptions. If you feel mentioned, look for supporting behaviour. Are people looking at you? Has anyone commented on you? Has anything changed in the environment? If the answer is no, the illusion likely formed from internal noise. You can remind yourself of this pattern.

Recognising this illusion does not eliminate it. It reduces its power. You still feel sensations, but you no longer treat them as messages. You understand that the brain dislikes uncertainty. You understand that the body reacts to possibility, not evidence. You understand that heat in your ear does not reveal anyone's thoughts.

The chapter that follows explains why three people can experience the same sensation and form different interpretations. Their backgrounds, beliefs and cultural frameworks shape their stories. You will see how environment and meaning build the next layer of this pattern.

10

The Teacher Who Felt Watched

The school hallway hummed with the usual morning noise. Students moved between lockers and classrooms. The air carried the sharp smell of disinfectant from the weekend cleaning. Louise held a stack of exercise books against her side as she walked towards her classroom. Her left ear felt warm. The heat rose slowly at first, then sharpened. She noticed it because she had no distractions yet. Her mind had not filled with tasks or conversations. The sensation stood out.

She had taught for fifteen years. She knew the routine. She knew the staff. She knew the rhythms of the school day. Yet some mornings still felt tense. She could not explain why. Her body reacted early on days when she felt unsure. She reached the classroom door and touched the metal handle. She paused. Her ear still felt warm. She told herself it was nothing, but the warmth lingered.

Inside the staffroom earlier that morning, she had entered just as two teachers lowered their voices. They were not close friends.

They spoke often enough to remain polite, but she never felt part of their group. They had been whispering with their backs turned. When they noticed her, they shifted their posture. The moment was small. Their reaction was mild. Yet her stomach tightened. She felt the first hint of discomfort. She pushed it aside and made coffee. She tried to act neutral, but the whisper stuck in her mind. It sat in the background for the rest of the morning.

Her body reacted more strongly than the situation demanded. She knew this pattern. She had experienced it before. When she felt insecure, her body produced signals that made ordinary interactions feel sharp. Kahneman describes this as fast emotional processing. The body reacts early. The story comes later. Louise knew the sequence well. She felt it often enough to recognise it, but she still struggled to manage it.

As she placed the exercise books on her desk, the warmth in her ear intensified. The feeling became noticeable enough that she touched the ear lightly. It felt normal to her hand. The heat came from inside. Her mind rushed to explain it. She pictured the two teachers in the staffroom. She replayed the whisper. She replayed the shift in posture. She wondered if she had been the topic.

The idea felt uncomfortable, but it also felt familiar. Louise had learned early in life to watch for signs of judgement. She grew up in a house where small mistakes triggered strong reactions. Her father corrected her often. He used short comments that stayed with her for days. Her mother avoided conflict, which pushed Louise to monitor every cue for risk. She learned to scan for changes in tone or expression. She learned to read silence as trouble. These habits followed her into adulthood.

Van der Kolk explains how early instability shapes a person's interpretation of social cues. The body stores reactions from the past. When a similar situation appears, the body reacts even if the present moment carries no real threat. Louise lived inside this pattern. Her body treated uncertainty as danger. The warmth in her ear felt like a warning. The whisper in the staffroom felt like further evidence.

The students entered the classroom. Chairs scraped. Bags dropped. The noise increased. Louise shifted her focus to the lesson. She felt calm enough to begin. She greeted the class and wrote the date on the board. She explained the morning activity. Her voice sounded steady. Her body felt less steady. The heat had moved from her ear to her cheeks. She ignored it as best she could.

Halfway through the lesson, two students exchanged a quiet laugh. They glanced in her direction. The laugh had nothing to do with her. The glance lasted a fraction of a second. Yet her chest tightened. She felt exposed. Critchley's work shows how anxiety increases interoceptive sensitivity. People feel small sensations more strongly. They attach meaning quickly. Louise recognised the effect. She felt it each time stress built without release.

She continued teaching. She corrected work. She answered questions. She kept her tone even. The class behaved well, but her attention drifted to her internal signals. Her ear warmed again. Her pulse quickened. She resisted the urge to check the doorway or the hallway. She knew these reactions came from within. She also knew the sensations pushed her towards interpretation. The mind dislikes sensation without meaning. It searches for explanation. Ariely describes this as the mind's attempt to reduce discomfort. Louise felt the discomfort spreading.

During the short break between sessions, she stepped into the hallway for air. She walked towards the staffroom to refill her water bottle. She passed two students who spoke quietly to each other. One student glanced at her. The glance felt quick and neutral, yet her body reacted. Her stomach tightened slightly. She felt a shift in her shoulders. She recognised the pattern, but she could not stop it. She sensed attention even when attention did not exist.

Inside the staffroom, the same two teachers from the morning stood near the counter. They spoke in low tones again. When they saw her, they straightened. They paused for a moment. The moment was small. It was a common behaviour. It should not have meant anything. Yet Louise felt a rush of heat to her face. Her ear warmed again. Her hands felt slightly cold. She filled her bottle. She forced a small smile. She walked out.

The social alarm system activates fast in moments like these. Sapolsky explains that the body reacts to possible social threat with the same circuits used for physical threat. Louise's body followed this rule. Her mind followed the sensation. The sensation convinced her that she had been noticed or judged. The illusion formed quickly. She felt mentioned even though nobody had said a word about her.

She tried to analyse the whisper. She tried to recall the tone. She wondered if she had done something recently that could prompt criticism. She replayed the previous week. She thought about interactions with students. She thought about meetings with parents. She struggled to find a reason. Her body told her a story. Her mind obeyed.

During the lunch break, she sat alone for several minutes. She opened her lunch container and tried to focus on eating. She chewed slowly, but her mind continued to run. She asked herself whether she had misread the cues. She asked herself whether the whispers were about work or something personal. She asked herself why her body reacted so strongly. She told herself she was overthinking. The warmth in her ear spread again. She lost trust in her reassurance.

A colleague named Marcus entered the staffroom and greeted her. He sat down across from her. He asked about her weekend. She responded politely. She liked Marcus. He never made her feel uneasy. His tone felt steady. He listened without judgement. She felt her body relax slightly during the conversation. Her shoulders loosened. Her cheeks cooled. For a moment, the alarm faded.

Marcus mentioned a planning meeting scheduled for later in the afternoon. Louise nodded. She made a note. Then he said something casual. He mentioned that he had seen two teachers speaking about a roster change earlier that morning. He said it in a neutral tone. The comment matched ordinary staffroom conversation. Yet Louise felt her chest tighten again. She linked his statement to her own assumptions. She believed he had unintentionally confirmed her fears.

She asked who the teachers were. Marcus named the same two who had whispered earlier. He continued speaking about the roster. He explained that one teacher wanted to swap a duty. The comment made sense. It had nothing to do with her. Yet her mind resisted the neutral explanation. The sensations felt too strong to ignore. She assumed the conversation he overheard involved her as well.

This interpretation came from her internal state, not the facts. De Becker's work highlights how people misread ordinary behaviour as threat when their internal alarm system activates. Louise sat inside that pattern. She struggled to reframe the morning. She wanted to accept the neutral explanation. The warmth in her ear made the explanation feel weak.

After lunch, she returned to her classroom. She prepared for the next lesson. She tried to focus, but her mind continued to work in the background. She convinced herself that the two teachers had changed their behaviour due to something she had done. She assumed the students' laughter reflected her. She assumed the glance from the hallway signalled judgement.

She picked up a textbook and placed it on the front table. She felt her palm sweat slightly. She took a slow breath. She reminded herself that students often laugh at unrelated jokes. She reminded herself that adults lower their voices for many reasons. She reminded herself that her body reacts strongly on days when she feels tired or stretched. These reminders helped briefly. The sensations returned whenever her attention drifted.

During the afternoon planning meeting, she sat near the middle of the room. The principal spoke about scheduling changes. The meeting moved quickly. People asked questions. People wrote notes. Louise participated calmly. She appeared steady to others. She contributed to a discussion about assessment deadlines. Her voice sounded confident.

Yet her body felt tight. She felt the heat rise again each time the two teachers spoke to each other. They sat several seats away. They whispered once in the middle of the meeting. It was a quick exchange. It had nothing to do with her. She could not hear the content. The whisper felt sharp anyway. Her ear warmed. Her mind filled the silence with stories. She believed the whisper related to her performance. She believed these teachers had discussed her earlier. She held this belief even though she had no evidence.

The meeting ended. People packed their papers and left. Louise walked out with her notebook pressed against her chest. Her steps felt stiff. She approached the car park and felt the late afternoon air settle on her skin. Her body cooled slightly. She reached her car and sat with her hands on the wheel. She allowed herself a moment to breathe.

She knew she had misread the day. She knew her reactions came from inside. She knew the sensations misled her. She also knew that these patterns ran deep. They came from childhood. They came from old experiences that shaped her interpretation of social cues. She understood the mechanics, yet she still reacted. The knowledge helped her but did not remove the instinct.

On the drive home, she replayed the day again. She questioned whether her teaching had changed recently. She questioned whether she had offended someone. She questioned whether she had been too quiet at staff events. She questioned more than she needed to. The questions came from the discomfort in her body, not from logic.

Louise reached home and changed into comfortable clothes. She made tea and sat on the couch. The warmth in her ear finally faded. The tension in her chest eased. She allowed herself to recognise the pattern. She felt embarrassed by the strength of her reactions. She felt confused by her body's speed. She felt worn down by the uncertainty. She wanted clarity.

She opened her laptop and read through materials on stress and interpretation. She had studied these topics before. She returned to them often because they gave her perspective. She reread a section from Critchley describing how anxiety increases the intensity of interoceptive signals. She reread a section from van der Kolk explaining how old experiences create strong bodily reactions to mild triggers. She reread notes on Kahneman's idea that fast interpretations form even when evidence is weak.

She closed the laptop and placed it on the table. She rested her head against the back of the couch. She felt calm enough to reflect. She realised that nothing in her day had confirmed her fears. The two teachers had spoken about a roster change, not about her. The students had laughed at something unrelated. The hallway glance meant nothing. The sensations came from within.

She understood the pattern more clearly. The warmth in her ear arrived first. The story came later. The story felt real because the sensation felt strong. Her mind built explanations that matched her fears. The explanations had no evidence. They grew from her body's automatic reactions.

She promised herself she would watch the pattern more carefully. She wanted to recognise the signs early. She wanted to separate sensation from story. She wanted to remind herself that her body reacts to possibility, not truth. She knew the instinct would not disappear. She knew the pattern would return. She hoped to handle it with more distance.

The next morning, she walked into the school with a calmer posture. She carried her books and greeted the office staff. She walked past the same teachers from the previous day. They smiled and said good morning. The tone felt warm and ordinary. Louise felt a small wave of relief. She realised that the narrative she built had no foundation. She understood how easily the mind creates stories from noise.

Louise's experience shows how social interpretation becomes distorted when the body reacts strongly. It shows how sensation drives meaning. It shows how uncertainty produces stories shaped by history, not fact. It shows how early experiences influence the present. It shows how easy it is to believe a sensation tells the truth.

The case also shows something more important. When people notice the pattern, they can separate the reaction from the story. They can see the difference between internal noise and external reality. They can understand why their bodies react before their minds can evaluate the situation. They can build a more grounded picture of the environment.

This separation becomes a key skill. It reduces unnecessary stress. It builds clarity. It weakens the illusion that others speak about you. It strengthens your sense of control. The next chapter shows how thoughts turn sensations into stories and why the mind struggles to resist this process when uncertainty rises.

Jason A. Solomon, B.Ed

PART IV

THE PSYCHOLOGY OF MEANING

Turning Sensation Into Story

Humans turn physical sensations into explanations with remarkable speed. A warm ear, a tight chest or a slight shift in breathing becomes a clue that something meaningful has happened. The body reacts first. The mind follows with a narrative. The process feels natural because it unfolds in seconds. It also feels convincing because the sensation appears before the thought. You trust the sensation. You treat the story as evidence even when nothing confirms it.

This habit runs through everyday life. People interpret sensations constantly. They feel a sudden change in temperature and assume it signals emotion. They feel pressure in their stomach and assume someone dislikes them. They notice heat in one ear and assume they have been mentioned. These interpretations come from fast cognitive processes. Kahneman explains that the mind produces instant conclusions because uncertainty feels unsafe. The body offers the raw material. The mind shapes it into a story.

The process begins with interoception. Interoception refers to the brain's ability to sense internal states. Craig's research shows that interoception gives humans continuous updates about their organs, muscles and skin. The brain receives information about temperature, tension, movement and pressure. Most signals stay below conscious awareness. Some rise to the surface because they appear sharp, sudden or unusual. When a sensation feels unfamiliar, the mind pays attention. It reacts by seeking meaning.

People dislike unexplained sensations. A sensation with no cause feels disruptive. Humans want order. They want stability. They want a sense of control. When the body delivers a strong signal, the mind searches for an anchor. It asks, "What caused this?" If the environment feels uncertain, the mind turns to social meaning. It assumes that someone else caused the sensation. This leap occurs because humans evolved to watch each other closely. Dunbar's research on social cognition shows how much time people spend tracking group behaviour and reputation.

The story often forms before logic intervenes. You walk into a room. You feel heat in your ear. At that moment, someone lowers their voice. You link the two events. You assume the sensation reflects the conversation. Your brain did not check the facts. It simply matched the timing. Kahneman calls this the coherence instinct. The brain prefers a complete story over a partial one. It builds explanations even when evidence is thin.

This pattern strengthens when people feel stressed. Stress increases sensitivity to internal signals. Critchley explains that anxious individuals feel sensations more intensely. Their nervous systems amplify normal physical processes. A mild increase in blood flow feels like heat. A normal muscle contraction feels like tension. A shift in breathing feels like danger. The mind interprets the sensations as meaningful because the sensations feel sharp.

People with unpredictable childhoods often read sensations through a lens of caution. Van der Kolk describes how early experiences shape the nervous system. If someone grew up in an environment where small cues signalled conflict, their body reacts strongly to uncertainty. They turned subtle sensations into warnings during childhood. These habits continue into adulthood. Their bodies deliver signals at the slightest change. Their minds interpret the signals as signs of judgement or threat.

Another factor drives this pattern. The brain confuses correlation with causation. If two events occur close together, the brain assumes one caused the other. This instinct once helped humans navigate dangerous environments. A rustle in the bush followed by movement signalled risk. Today the same instinct misfires in social settings. A warm ear followed by a quiet pause feels like a connection even though the two events do not relate.

People also rely on emotional reasoning. Emotional reasoning occurs when someone believes something is true because it feels true. The body creates a strong sensation. The sensation creates discomfort. The discomfort produces a belief. The belief feels real because the sensation felt real. Kahneman notes that emotional reasoning overrides logic because emotion appears first. Emotion captures attention. Logic arrives later.

This pattern grows stronger when identity feels uncertain. Humans want to understand how others see them. They want to maintain social standing. They want to feel valued. When these needs feel fragile, sensations become tools for prediction. People assume their bodies reveal how others view them. They treat heat, tension or tightness as signals of social relevance. These interpretations reflect the desire to feel seen and secure.

Projection adds another layer. People project their fears onto sensations. If they fear criticism, they interpret sensations as signs of criticism. If they fear exclusion, they interpret sensations as signs of exclusion. Ariely shows how humans seek patterns that support their internal beliefs. Sensations become evidence for these beliefs.

People forget that they supplied the belief before they supplied the meaning.

The narrative instinct shapes the final step. Humans create stories to explain their experiences. They link events into sequences. They add intention where none exists. They ignore information that contradicts the story. This instinct helped humans learn from the past. It also helped them predict future events. Today it creates issues when sensations form without cause. The mind still builds a story even when no story exists.

Consider a simple scene. Someone leaves a meeting. Their shoulders feel tight. Their ear warms. They assume the tension reflects how others saw their performance. They replay comments. They replay tone. They ignore the possibility that the sensation came from hunger, temperature or fatigue. The sensation felt personal. The story followed the feeling.

Another example appears in dating. A person waits for a message from someone they like. Their chest feels tight. Their ear warms. They assume the sensation reflects a shift in the relationship. They read tone into silence. They use sensation to interpret uncertainty. They forget that the sensation arose because of their anxiety, not because of the other person.

This pattern also appears in workplaces. Someone walks past a group of colleagues who stop speaking. Their ear warms. They assume the conversation involved them. They treat the warmth as a social signal. They forget that blood flow increases during mild stress. Their mind matches the physiology to the environment without checking facts.

The process repeats in schools. A teenager feels heat in their face. Two classmates whisper nearby. The teenager assumes the whisper relates to them. Their body reacts strongly due to hormonal shifts. Their mind assigns the cause to peers. The story forms because the sensation felt personal.

All these examples share the same structure. Sensation arrives first. Interpretation follows. The interpretation depends on past experiences, identity, stress and emotional state. The interpretation often reflects internal fears rather than external events.

People struggle to break this pattern because the sensations feel so convincing. When the body reacts, the mind accepts the reaction as evidence. The mind forgets that sensations can arise from temperature, hormones, digestion, movement or random neural activity. The mind wants meaning. It searches for it even when nothing meaningful occurred.

Awareness helps reduce this pattern. You can learn to recognise the sequence. You can pause when a sensation appears. You can ask whether anything in the environment supports the interpretation. You can check the facts. You can notice when your body reacts to stress rather than to actual events. You can identify when the story came from fear rather than evidence.

People often misinterpret sensations because they assign them to others. They want to explain how they feel. They want to understand their place in the group. They use the fastest tools available. The fastest tool is a sensation. The fastest explanation is a social story. The combination feels true. It feels grounded. It carries emotional weight. It carries narrative weight. It does not always carry accuracy.

You can reshape your response by recognising that your body reacts to many factors at once. You may feel heat because you moved quickly. You may feel tension because you slept poorly. You may feel pressure because you worked through a stressful week. You may feel warmth in your ear because blood flow increased for reasons unrelated to social interaction.

Once you learn to separate the sensation from the story, you weaken the illusion that bodily signals reveal hidden judgement. You begin to see the difference between internal processes and external events. You learn to test your assumptions. You learn to pause before forming conclusions. You learn to question the link between sensation and meaning.

Craig's work on interoception supports this approach. He shows that people who pay clear attention to internal states without adding interpretations develop better emotional regulation. They observe sensations without assigning stories. They recognise when their bodies react for ordinary reasons. They feel more grounded.

Kahneman's research adds another layer. He explains that fast thinking is useful but often inaccurate. Slowing down improves accuracy. Slowing down lets logic catch up. Slowing down breaks the link between sensation and automatic narrative.

Aronson's work shows that self concept remains sensitive to feedback. People struggle when they feel judged. Recognising the difference between internal signals and external judgement protects self worth.

Van der Kolk's work shows how old patterns influence current interpretation. When people understand their history, they understand their reactions. They stop blaming themselves for instinctive sensations.

Ariely's research highlights how humans use emotion to fill gaps in information. Understanding this process helps people identify when emotions shape the story, not facts.

When you apply these insights, you form a clearer relationship with your body. You notice sensations. You recognise patterns. You understand that sensation does not equal truth. You understand that stories built from discomfort often reflect fear rather than fact.

This chapter shows how the mind turns sensation into meaning. The process is quick. The process is natural. The process is not always accurate. When you see the sequence, you can step outside it.

The next chapter explores why the need to feel seen influences this pattern. You will see how identity, attention and validation shape the stories people create from ordinary sensations.

The Human Need to Feel Seen

Humans want to feel noticed. They want to feel valued. They want to feel recognised by the people around them. This need begins early in life and continues through adulthood. It shapes behaviour in families, workplaces, friendships and intimate relationships. It also shapes how people interpret bodily sensations. A warm ear, a shift in breathing or tension in the chest can feel like a sign that someone else has noticed you. The body reacts. The mind creates a meaning. The meaning often reflects the desire for visibility.

Recognition plays a central role in identity. Aronson's work on self concept shows that people build their sense of self from feedback. They watch how others respond. They track approval and disapproval. They monitor cues that reveal acceptance. When humans feel seen, they feel stable. When they feel ignored, they feel unsettled. This desire for recognition shapes the stories people tell themselves when their bodies react.

Children learn the importance of recognition from caregivers. A child who receives consistent attention learns that they matter. A child who receives inconsistent attention learns to monitor every cue for signs of interest. Children who fear losing connection become sensitive to changes in tone, posture or mood. They search for signs that someone cares. This habit follows them into later life. Their bodies react strongly to minor changes because visibility feels linked to safety.

A teenager carries this pattern into school environments. They enter classrooms where social approval shapes belonging. They track every glance and comment. They watch how peers respond. They want to feel part of the group. When they feel heat rise in their face or ears, they assume the sensation reflects how others see them. The sensation becomes a sign of visibility. The interpretation reflects their need for relevance in a shifting social world.

Young adults experience the same pattern in workplaces. They want to prove themselves. They want to earn respect. They want to establish their place in the organisation. When they feel tension in their body during meetings, they assume the tension reflects others' judgement. They treat the sensation as a cue that someone has formed an opinion about them. The interpretation grows from the desire to know where they stand.

Adults in intimate relationships carry the pattern forward. They watch their partner's reactions. They monitor tone. They track subtle shifts in behaviour. They want reassurance. They want attention. When their body reacts, they often interpret the reaction through the lens of attachment. A warm ear becomes a sign of emotional distance or closeness. A shift in breathing becomes a sign of tension. The body delivers a sensation. The mind links it to relationship stability.

Older adults also experience the need to feel seen. They want to feel relevant in families, communities and friendships. They watch how people respond to them. They track whether younger relatives listen, whether friends include them and whether colleagues respect their input. When they feel sudden warmth or subtle tension, they may treat the sensation as a signal that someone has shifted their perception of them. They interpret the sensation through their desire to maintain social value.

The need to feel seen explains why humans personalise sensations. They assign meaning based on relevance. If someone feels invisible, they interpret a sensation as a sign of being noticed. If someone feels judged, they interpret the sensation as confirmation. This habit forms from the desire to understand how others view them.

Craig's research on interoception shows that bodily sensations become part of emotional understanding. They shape how people interpret social cues. When someone wants recognition, their body reacts strongly to small shifts in the environment. The mind uses these sensations as evidence. The mind assumes the sensation reveals social truth.

This pattern becomes stronger when people feel uncertain. If someone doubts their value at work, they interpret sensations as signals of disapproval. If someone feels insecure in a relationship, they interpret sensations as signs of conflict. If someone feels overlooked socially, they interpret sensations as signs that others have finally acknowledged them. The sensation becomes a tool to support the fear or the hope.

Several psychological processes shape this habit. One is personal relevance. Humans prioritise information that relates to them. If a sensation feels personal, the mind interprets it through the lens of self. People assume others are focused on them. They forget that most people think about their own concerns. Aronson highlights this bias in discussions on self awareness. People overestimate how much others notice them. This bias makes bodily sensations feel socially significant.

Another process is confirmation seeking. People search for cues that match their inner beliefs. Ariely explains that humans want consistency. If someone believes they are being ignored, they look for evidence. A sensation becomes a clue. If someone believes they are being judged, they treat sensations as confirmation. They ignore alternative explanations. They trust their internal signals even when the signals form from stress or fatigue.

Emotional hunger adds further intensity. People want attention. They want connection. They want proof that others care. When social attention feels scarce, sensations fill the gap. A person may interpret a warm ear as proof that someone discussed them. They accept the idea because the alternative feels empty. Humans want acknowledgement. They sometimes create it from internal signals.

Fear of invisibility also shapes this pattern. Being unnoticed feels uncomfortable. Humans want to contribute. They want to matter. They want recognition. When someone feels peripheral, they may treat sensations as signs that someone finally noticed them. A small cue becomes meaningful. The sensation becomes a sign that they are relevant again.

Another factor involves social comparison. Humans compare themselves to peers. They want to feel competent. They want to feel valued. They want to feel included. When comparison leaves them unsure, they interpret sensations as signals that others have formed opinions. A slight flush becomes evidence. A small tension becomes a sign of evaluation. The mind attaches social meaning to sensations because comparison increases sensitivity.

The desire for visibility also influences how people create stories from silence. Silence feels uncertain. People want feedback. They want clarity. When silence appears, they rely on sensations to fill the gap. They interpret sensations as signs of what others might think. They forget that silence often has no social meaning. The interpretation reflects their internal need, not the external reality.

Dunbar's work shows how much time humans spend thinking about their social position. They maintain awareness of status, alliances and group dynamics. They consider how others see them. They notice cues that reveal acceptance. This constant awareness makes sensations feel socially relevant. A warm ear appears at the same moment someone looks away. The mind links the two events. The link forms from the desire to understand social standing.

Attachment patterns influence this behaviour. People with secure attachment interpret sensations calmly. People with anxious attachment interpret sensations through fear. They assume someone has shifted their opinion. They assume someone has judged them. They treat sensations as social indicators. Their history shapes their interpretation.

Stress increases the intensity. Sapolsky explains that stress sensitises the body to internal signals. When someone experiences stress, sensations feel sharp. Sharp sensations demand meaning. The mind turns to social interpretation because social meaning matters. The body reacts to internal strain. The mind interprets the reaction as external judgement.

Workplaces offer countless examples. A person presents in a meeting. Their ear warms halfway through. They assume someone disliked their idea. They scan faces. They search for cues. They link the sensation to imagined reactions. They forget that stress can shift blood flow for reasons unrelated to the audience.

Families show similar patterns. A person attends a gathering. They feel a sudden flush. They interpret the flush as a sign that someone judged them or discussed them earlier. They search the room. They analyse tone. They treat the sensation as evidence of social tension.

Friendships contain the same dynamic. Someone meets a friend after a period of silence. Their body reacts with heat or tension. They assume the friend feels distant or critical. They build a story around the sensation. The story forms from internal uncertainty, not external behaviour.

Digital communication heightens this pattern. People search for signs of attention in messages, posts and reactions. They want to feel noticed. When communication slows or lacks clarity, sensations fill the gap. A warm ear becomes a signal of attention. A tight chest becomes a signal of judgement. Turkle's work on digital behaviour shows how online environments increase the desire for recognition. People rely on internal cues to interpret unclear messages.

This need for visibility shapes how people experience bodily sensations. It increases the likelihood that they will treat sensations as signals of social relevance. They interpret heat or tension as messages from others. They forget that the body produces sensations constantly. They forget that most sensations reflect internal processes. They forget that social meaning often forms without evidence.

Awareness helps change this pattern. People can learn to notice when their need for recognition drives their interpretation. They can ask whether the sensation reflects internal emotion or external feedback. They can separate self worth from momentary signals. They can check the environment before assuming meaning. They can learn to pause when sensations appear.

Understanding the need to feel seen reduces the power of bodily illusions. It helps people recognise when their desire for relevance shapes their stories. It helps them understand that sensation does not reveal social truth. It shows them how their internal needs influence their perception.

When people recognise this pattern, they can slow the process. They can observe sensations without building narratives. They can separate internal states from external events. They can direct their attention to evidence rather than assumptions.

The next chapter explains why people use superstition as an emotional shortcut and how simple stories help them reduce uncertainty when sensations appear without clear cause.

Superstition as Emotional Shortcuts

Humans prefer simple explanations when they face uncertainty. They want answers that reduce discomfort. They want clarity when the body behaves in unexpected ways. Superstition fills this gap. It offers quick meaning when sensations appear without warning. People do not choose superstition because they lack intelligence. They choose it because it gives emotional relief. It acts as a shortcut that reduces confusion. Frazer describes this tendency in his work on cultural beliefs. He shows how people across different societies use symbolic stories to manage uncertainty.

When sensations feel strange, the mind seeks structure. A sudden rise of heat in the ears or a tight feeling in the chest disrupts the sense of stability. These sensations demand interpretation. They demand context. Humans dislike unexplained signals. The instinct for explanation arrives before careful thought. Kahneman explains that fast thinking takes over in moments of ambiguity. Fast thinking relies on habit and intuition. It draws from cultural beliefs, personal fears and familiar stories.

Superstition offers fast answers that feel satisfying. It reduces the pressure to analyse. It gives the mind something to hold. Radford's work on folklore shows that people rely on superstition because it lowers emotional load. When a sensation feels uncomfortable, a simple explanation protects the person from sitting with uncertainty. The explanation may not be accurate, but it feels safe.

Bodily sensations provide fertile ground for superstition. The body shifts without notice. It produces heat, cold, tension and pressure for many reasons. Hormones change. Blood flow shifts. Muscles contract. Nerves fire. Digestive processes fluctuate. Interoception brings some of these signals into awareness. Craig explains that interoception influences emotional responses. When sensations feel unusual, they demand meaning. People search for the quickest story available. Superstition supplies it.

History supports this pattern. Early communities lacked scientific tools. They used symbolic reasoning to explain physical experiences. If a person felt heat in the ear, they assumed someone mentioned them. If a person felt their eye twitch, they assumed a message awaited them. If a person felt a shiver, they believed a spirit passed near them. These explanations reduced fear. They made sensations feel organised. Frazer documents these patterns across global traditions. He shows that people relied on simple stories because they helped them cope.

Modern humans face similar instincts. Even with scientific knowledge, they still prefer fast explanations during stress. A warm ear may be interpreted as a sign of gossip. A tight stomach may be interpreted as a sign of social conflict. A hollow feeling in the chest may be interpreted as a sign of rejection. These interpretations feel intuitive because they match emotional expectations. They reduce uncertainty. They give structure to discomfort.

Superstition also offers social value. It creates a shared language. When people use common sayings to explain sensations, they reinforce group identity. These sayings create continuity between generations. They give people a sense of cultural stability. Dunbar's work highlights how shared beliefs strengthen social bonds. Even when the belief lacks factual grounding, it brings people together.

The desire for belonging strengthens superstition. When someone feels isolated, simple explanations provide comfort. They support the idea that others think about them. They reduce the discomfort of invisibility. Superstitions about bodily sensations often reflect the desire to feel connected. If someone feels ignored, they may interpret a sensation as proof that others still notice them. The interpretation offers emotional relief.

Superstitions also simplify emotional experiences. When people cannot identify the source of a feeling, they turn to symbolic meaning. This process reduces cognitive load. Ariely explains that humans use simplified rules to manage complex information. When faced with unclear signals, they choose explanations that require minimal effort. Superstitions offer these explanations.

For example, someone feels heat in one ear while walking home. They do not stop to evaluate their stress level, body temperature, fatigue or recent conversations. They choose the quickest explanation. They assume someone has mentioned them. The explanation fits a familiar cultural script. It requires no analysis. It reduces uncertainty at once. The mind accepts it.

Another example appears in workplaces. A person enters a meeting room and feels a sudden shift in their stomach. The sensation may arise from hunger or preparation for public speaking. The person interprets the sensation as a sign that others disapprove of them. This interpretation matches their emotional state. Superstition becomes a tool for emotional certainty.

Students use similar shortcuts. A teenager feels heat in their cheeks during a school assembly. They assume someone in the crowd noticed them. They rely on superstition to manage social tension.

The explanation feels easier than examining their stress. It reduces the discomfort of not knowing.

Older adults rely on these shortcuts as well. A sudden sensation during a family event may be interpreted through cultural or generational beliefs. The sensation becomes a sign of attention or significance. The interpretation helps the person feel connected to long-standing traditions. It offers a sense of continuity.

These patterns reveal that superstition acts as a form of emotional regulation. People use it to manage discomfort. They may not recognise it consciously. They may not name it. The system operates beneath awareness. It emerges in moments of uncertainty. It appears when people seek psychological comfort.

Superstitions persist because they are simple. They rely on clear rules. They do not require deep thought. They match emotional needs. They remain stable across time because they help people manage internal confusion. Radford notes that beliefs survive when they offer emotional value. Bodily superstitions survive because they support emotional stability.

The brain also contributes to the endurance of superstition. Humans notice patterns even when patterns do not exist. Kahneman describes this as automatic pattern recognition. When someone experiences a sensation at the same moment they hear a whisper, they assume a connection. The brain links the events. The link feels valid because it forms quickly. The mind repeats the connection in future moments. The repetition strengthens the belief.

Culture reinforces these patterns. Families teach children to interpret bodily sensations through shared beliefs. Communities pass these sayings across generations. They become part of everyday language. They feel natural because they are familiar. People accept them long before they question them.

The simplicity of these beliefs protects them. A person who feels heat in their ear does not need to examine blood flow, temperature, stress levels or context. They repeat a familiar phrase. The phrase offers comfort. It stops the questioning process. It provides closure.

This tendency becomes stronger when someone faces stress. Sapolsky explains that stress reduces the ability to think clearly. Stress pushes people towards automatic habits. Superstition operates as one of these habits. It saves cognitive resources. It avoids deeper emotional work. It helps people cope quickly.

Superstition also thrives during transitions. When someone begins a new job, enters a new social environment or faces change, sensations rise. The mind interprets these sensations as signs of hidden meaning. They rely on simple explanations because their emotional state feels fragile.

Some people treat these beliefs light-heartedly. They joke about a warm ear or a twitching eyelid. Others use them seriously. They attach strong meaning to small cues. Their emotional state determines how deeply they rely on superstition. People facing uncertainty lean harder on symbolic shortcuts. People feeling secure treat them as harmless sayings.

Superstitions about bodily sensations reveal something important about human behaviour. They show how people respond when they cannot find clear explanations. They show how emotion drives interpretation. They show how the desire for clarity shapes beliefs. They show how cultural habits influence perception.

When someone recognises these patterns, they can reduce their reliance on superstition. They can pause when a sensation appears. They can ask themselves whether the explanation reflects evidence or comfort. They can examine whether the sensation came from stress, fatigue or temperature. They can become aware of their desire for simplicity.

Awareness weakens the shortcut. It does not remove it completely. It reduces its power. It helps people separate emotion from interpretation. It helps people make decisions based on evidence rather than habit. It strengthens clarity.

Superstition remains part of human psychology because it addresses emotional needs. It reduces fear. It offers quick meaning. It provides a sense of order. These benefits kept it alive across centuries. Even today, with scientific understanding, superstition appears whenever people face uncertainty. It appears when sensations feel personal. It appears when clarity feels distant.

This chapter shows why humans rely on symbolic shortcuts when interpreting bodily sensations. The next chapter moves from theory to practice. It provides tools to help readers recognise their triggers and reduce misinterpretation in daily life.

14

Reflection Exercise:

When You Think Others Are Talking About You

Humans often react to bodily sensations as if they contain hidden messages. A warm ear, a tight chest or a sudden shift in breathing can trigger quick interpretations about what others think or say. These interpretations grow from instinct, memory and emotion. They feel convincing because the body reacts before the mind can assess the situation. This chapter offers tools to break that cycle. It guides you through practical exercises that help you separate sensation from interpretation. It also helps you recognise the triggers that shape your assumptions.

These exercises draw on research from Damasio, Ariely, Craig and other scholars who explain how the brain blends internal signals with emotional meaning. They show how slow reflection reduces the errors that follow automatic interpretations. They also show how clarity grows when people observe sensations without attaching stories to them.

This chapter does not aim to remove your reactions. It aims to help you understand them. When you understand them, you reduce the power of false beliefs. You recognise when your body signals stress rather than social judgement. You notice when your mind fills gaps with assumptions rather than evidence. You learn to slow the sequence that leads from sensation to story.

BODY MAPPING FOR CLARITY

Body mapping helps you identify where you feel sensations during social discomfort. People often sense patterns without noticing them. They feel changes in their chest, stomach, neck or ears. They treat each change as a message rather than a normal biological response. When you map these sensations, you see how predictable they are. You recognise that the body reacts in the same places at the same moments. You notice how often the reactions appear in unrelated situations.

Start by sitting comfortably. Let your breathing settle. Pay attention to your internal state for several moments. Do not analyse. Simply observe. Craig explains that interoceptive attention improves emotional understanding. You do not need to label the sensations. You only need to register them.

Recall a recent moment when you believed someone talked about you. Picture the environment. Picture the tone. Picture the faces. Notice what your body did. Notice where the first signal appeared. Many people feel heat in their ears or face. Others feel tension across their chest. Others feel pressure in their stomach. Identify your first signal.

Then recall the next signal. Did your shoulders tighten. Did your breathing shift. Did your hands cool. Did your pulse rise. Trace the sequence. The sequence reveals your personal pattern. Once you see it, you recognise it in future situations. The pattern helps you separate internal processes from social cues.

Write down the locations of the sensations. Write down their order. Write down what you assumed in the moment. This exercise makes the pattern visible. Once visible, it loses some of its ambiguity. Ambiguity fuels misinterpretation. Clarity reduces it.

IDENTIFYING TRIGGERS

Triggers occur before sensations. They appear quickly. They often remain unnoticed because they seem small. A quiet room, a shift in tone or a sideways glance can activate your social alarm system. The body reacts. You treat the reaction as social information. When you identify triggers, you interrupt the sequence much earlier. You catch the process before it gains strength.

Think of five recent moments when you felt sure someone talked about you. Write down what happened immediately before the sensation. Look for patterns. Did someone pause. Did someone whisper. Did you enter a room during a conversation. Did your day already feel stressful.

Sapolsky explains that stress amplifies internal signals. On stressful days, the body reacts more strongly to mild cues. Recognising this pattern helps you see when your interpretation forms from your own fatigue rather than external events.

Consider whether your triggers relate to memory. Van der Kolk shows how the body responds to reminders of past experiences. You may react strongly to environments that resemble earlier situations. You may react to tones that echo past criticism. When you identify these patterns, you understand why some moments feel heavier than others.

Write down each trigger. Beside it, write whether the trigger reflected evidence or assumption. If someone paused, ask whether pauses appear in many conversations. If someone looked away, ask whether people look away often while thinking. This step reveals the neutrality of many cues that once felt significant.

SENSATION VERSUS INTERPRETATION WORKSHEET

Separating sensation from interpretation requires deliberate effort. The body produces signals constantly. The mind interprets them automatically. Kahneman explains that the mind uses fast thinking when it feels uncertain. Fast thinking forms narratives quickly. Slow thinking requires intention. This exercise slows the process.

Create two columns. Label one column "Sensation". Label the other "Interpretation".

In the sensation column, list the physical signals you felt in a recent moment. Keep the language precise. Write "heat in left ear", "tightness in chest", "faster breathing", "stomach pressure", "shoulders raised". Avoid emotional labels. Describe only the physical change.

In the interpretation column, write the story you attached to the sensation. For example, "They criticised me", "They noticed something about me", "They whispered about my behaviour", "They judged my performance". This step reveals how quickly the mind builds meaning.

Now cross out any interpretation that lacks evidence. Evidence means you heard a comment, saw a clear expression or received direct feedback. If no evidence exists, the interpretation belongs to instinct rather than fact.

This worksheet trains you to treat sensations and interpretations as separate events. Once separated, they become easier to manage.

EMOTIONAL GROUNDING

Emotional grounding reduces the intensity of automatic reactions. It helps the body settle before the mind creates meaning. When the body calms, the interpretation weakens. Critchley notes that emotional grounding improves interoceptive accuracy. You feel the same sensations, but you interpret them more clearly.

Sit comfortably. Place your feet flat on the floor.

- Notice where your body connects with the chair.
- Notice the weight of your hands.

Breathe slowly with a rhythm that feels comfortable. Focus on the physical environment.

- Notice temperature.
- Notice sound.
- Notice the texture of your clothing.

This process returns attention to immediate reality. It reduces the influence of old patterns. It helps you recognise that sensations can arise without social cause. Repeat this technique during moments when you feel observed or mentioned. The technique interrupts the automatic story.

INTERRUPTING THE LOOP

People often follow a predictable loop. Sensation leads to interpretation. Interpretation leads to emotion. Emotion reinforces the interpretation.

The body reacts again. The loop repeats. Ariely explains that once a belief forms, people favour information that supports it. This keeps the loop active.

To interrupt the loop, insert questions between sensation and interpretation.

Ask:

- "Did I hear anything about me."
- "Did anyone mention my name."
- "Did anyone act differently towards me."
- "Does this sensation appear during unrelated stress."

These questions slow the pattern. They introduce logic. Logic competes with instinct. Kahneman notes that logical processing takes time. The loop relies on speed. Once slowed, it loses strength.

REFRAMING TOOLS

Reframing changes the meaning attached to a sensation. The sensation stays the same. The interpretation shifts. This technique does not attempt to remove your reaction. It aims to guide your understanding.

- When you feel heat in your ear, reframe it as a shift in blood flow.
- When you feel tension in your chest, reframe it as a stress signal.
- When you feel pressure in your stomach, reframe it as a normal physiological process.

These frames match the science. They align with Craig's explanation of interoception. They redirect your interpretation towards internal causes. The accuracy of these frames reduces the need for social explanations.

INTEROCEPTION DRILLS

Interoception drills help you build awareness without interpretation. They strengthen your ability to observe sensations calmly. Over time, they reduce misinterpretation.

Spend one minute each day noticing sensations across your body. Move your attention slowly from head to toe. Do not assign meaning. Simply notice temperature, movement or pressure.

Damasio explains that humans feel emotion through body signals. When you learn to observe the signals without building a narrative, you gain control over the emotional response. You can experience the sensation without attaching stories to it.

APPLYING THE EXERCISES TO REAL SITUATIONS

These tools work best when used consistently. Choose one environment where you often misinterpret sensations. It might be a workplace, social event or family gathering. Use the exercises during or after the event.

Notice your first reaction. Identify the sensation. Write down the interpretation. Test the interpretation against evidence. Use grounding if the sensation feels sharp. Use reframing if the narrative begins to form.

Over time, the pattern becomes easier to recognise. You learn that the body reacts for many reasons. You learn that sensations often reflect internal processes rather than external judgement. You learn to trust evidence more than instinct.

This chapter helps you understand how sensations gain meaning. It gives you tools to break automatic interpretations. It guides you to observe your internal state with clarity. It shows you that your body and mind do not always speak the same language. When you separate sensation from story, you reduce the pull of old patterns.

The next chapter moves from personal exercises to cultural patterns. It explains how different societies interpret the same sensations in different ways and why these interpretations endure across generations.

PART V

CULTURAL ECHOES AND GLOBAL BELIEFS

Idioms Across Cultures

Humans across the world created sayings that connect bodily sensations with social meaning. These sayings formed inside different environments, different belief systems and different historical pressures. They appear different on the surface, yet they follow the same pattern. People felt a sensation. They searched for meaning. They explained the sensation through social, spiritual or symbolic language. These explanations became idioms. The idioms survived because they offered emotional clarity when the body produced signals without warning.

Frazer and Radford document these patterns across many cultures. Their work shows that the interpretation of bodily sensations often follows predictable themes. Heat, tingling, twitching or pressure become signs of attention, danger or spiritual influence. These interpretations begin as assumptions. They become community customs. Over time they become fixed expressions passed across generations.

This chapter explores these traditions. It examines the beliefs found in Chinese, Indian, African, Celtic, Mediterranean, Middle Eastern and Latin cultures. It also explains why cultures that never interacted created similar interpretations. The similarities reveal something about human psychology. People respond to uncertainty in the same way regardless of geography. They want simple answers. They want emotional relief. They want stories that turn sensations into signs.

CHINESE TRADITIONS: CHEEKS, EARS AND SIGNS OF ATTENTION

Chinese communities have long interpreted bodily sensations as meaningful. A common belief links cheek warmth to someone mentioning you. Right cheek warmth can be seen as praise. Left cheek warmth can be viewed as criticism. This pattern mirrors the Roman separation between positive and negative mention. The two cultures developed these explanations independently. Both linked bodily asymmetry with social meaning. This shows how easily the mind matches physical sensations with symbolic direction.

Chinese traditions also link eye twitching to specific outcomes. The meaning shifts depending on the eye and the time of day. Frazer notes that people relied on these detailed rules to give structure to unpredictable sensations. A twitch that appears without warning feels intrusive. A detailed rulebook reduces uncertainty.

Heat in the ears appears in Chinese folklore as well. The belief frames heat as a social signal. The person becomes aware of the body through interoception. They want context. Tradition supplies it. This pattern fits Radford's analysis of idioms as tools for emotional organisation.

INDIAN BELIEFS: ASTROLOGY AND OMENS

Indian interpretations draw heavily from astrology. Many families treat bodily sensations as signs influenced by planetary movements. A sudden shift in body temperature or twitching in a particular area can be interpreted as an omen. The meaning changes with the position of the moon or the alignment of planets. These explanations connect the body to a larger cosmic system. They offer comfort by linking personal experiences to a structured universe.

These beliefs appear across regions of India with different variations. Some communities treat tingling in the left arm as a warning. Others view tingling in the right palm as a sign of incoming money. Heat in the ears can be seen as a sign that others discuss the person. These interpretations provide quick, culturally familiar answers.

Ariely notes that humans prefer explanations that reduce complexity. Astrology offers fixed rules. Rules reduce emotional load. They help people avoid long periods of uncertainty. In Indian traditions, bodily signs fit smoothly into this system.

AFRICAN TRADITIONS: SPIRITUAL SIGNALS AND SOCIAL MEANING

African communities across Nigeria, Ghana, Kenya and other regions also interpret bodily sensations within structured belief systems. Yoruba and Igbo traditions connect sensations to both social events and spiritual influences. A sudden warmth in a body part can be interpreted as a sign that someone speaks your name. The direction of the sensation matters. Heat on the left side can reflect conflict. Heat on the right can reflect praise or positive attention.

Some communities link tingling or twitching to ancestors or protective spirits. These interpretations reflect cultural views about unseen forces. They also reflect the importance of community perception. Dunbar's work on group size explains why humans remain sensitive to social judgement. African idioms reflect this sensitivity by framing sensations as signs of communal awareness.

Radford points out that these beliefs endure because they provide emotional reassurance. When people feel uncertain about their place in a group, idioms create a sense of connection. The sensation becomes a sign that others still think about them. The belief eases social tension.

CELTIC AND MEDITERRANEAN BELIEFS: SIGNS, OMENS AND WHISPERS

Celtic communities linked bodily sensations to the presence of unseen forces. A sudden flush in the ear or cheek could be interpreted as a sign that someone thought about you. A twitch in the hand or foot could signal upcoming visitors. These interpretations helped people understand random moments. They reduced the fear that came with unexplained sensations.

Mediterranean communities also built strong idioms around bodily heat. Greek households have a long tradition of linking ear warmth to gossip. Italian families share a similar belief. These traditions frame attention as both personal and social. People expect others to discuss them. The body becomes a receiver for that attention.

Frazer notes that Mediterranean cultures relied on symbolic interpretation because it helped them navigate close social environments. Families lived in tight quarters. Communities stayed interconnected. Social feedback mattered. Bodily sensations became tools for predicting shifts in relationships.

MIDDLE EASTERN BELIEFS: SIGNS OF PRESENCE AND SOCIAL ATTENTION

Middle Eastern communities developed idioms that connect bodily sensations with spiritual presence and social mention. Heat in the ears may signal that someone discusses you. Twitching in the eye or arm may signal incoming visitors or positive news. These interpretations vary across regions, yet they share the same core theme. They treat random sensations as signals of attention.

Some traditions link specific sensations to prayer or reflection. If someone experiences heat in the chest or face during contemplation, they may interpret it as a sign of alignment or insight. These beliefs reflect cultural values that connect the physical body to spiritual life. Radford notes that these systems remain stable because they help people frame internal signals through meaningful narratives.

LATIN TRADITIONS: GOSSIP, PRAISE AND PREDICTIONS

Many Latin cultures share a belief that sudden ear warmth signals gossip. In some regions, right ear warmth signals praise. Left ear warmth signals criticism. This pattern mirrors Roman and European interpretations. These cultural scripts passed through centuries because they support social cohesion. They help people understand their relationships. They offer simple explanations for unpredictable sensations.

Latin communities also link tingling palms or twitching legs to financial or social predictions. These idioms survive because they provide comfort during uncertainty. They reduce emotional confusion. They give structure to sensations that would otherwise feel random.

Jason A. Solomon, B.Ed

WHY CULTURES CREATED SIMILAR BELIEFS

The similarities across cultures reveal a deep psychological pattern. People from different continents created nearly identical explanations for bodily sensations even without contact. This pattern supports Kahneman's view that the mind seeks quick meaning. It also supports Craig's work on interoception, which shows that bodily awareness can feel unclear or intrusive. When the body behaves unpredictably, the mind seeks simple stories.

Frazer's research on symbolism shows that cultural meanings often develop from universal human concerns. People want safety. They want social clarity. They want control. They want to reduce uncertainty. Idioms give them these advantages. They offer ready-made explanations. They reduce the burden of confusion.

Radford highlights that idioms survive when they feel useful. Bodily idioms remain useful because sensations remain unpredictable. People want structures that organise their internal experiences. Idioms act as these structures.

SOCIAL VALUE OF SHARED IDIOMS

Idioms also shape social identity. Families use them to teach children how to interpret experiences. Communities use them to reinforce cultural values. Adults use them to connect with older generations. These sayings also offer comfort during stress. They support a sense of belonging.

Dunbar highlights the importance of shared stories for group cohesion. Idioms act as shared stories. They help people trust one another. They help people feel understood. They help people manage uncertainty together. This shared understanding strengthens emotional bonds.

WHY THESE SAYINGS SURVIVE IN MODERN LIFE

Modern science can explain every sensation listed in these idioms. Heat in the ear results from blood flow. Tingling results from nerves or circulation. Twitching results from muscle signals or fatigue. Despite this knowledge, the idioms remain active. They survive because they offer something science cannot replace. They offer emotional clarity in moments when people feel vulnerable.

Humans use these sayings as shortcuts. When someone feels heat in their ear, they repeat a familiar phrase. The phrase resolves uncertainty. It allows the person to move forward. Kahneman explains that humans prefer certainty over accuracy. Superstitions and idioms survive because they satisfy this preference.

GLOBAL PARALLELS REVEAL UNIVERSAL PSYCHOLOGY

The striking similarities between these cultural beliefs show that humans respond to bodily uncertainty in consistent ways. They assign meaning to sensations. They create stories to explain them. They spread these stories across generations. They rely on them during stress or confusion.

These idioms do not reflect ignorance. They reflect human psychology. They reveal how people manage fear, uncertainty and social tension. They show how culture helps the mind organise internal chaos.

As you move into the next chapter, you will see why these beliefs survive across centuries and why they remain powerful even when scientific explanations exist. The persistence of these idioms reveals something fundamental about how humans think, interpret and seek comfort in the face of the unknown.

16

Why These Beliefs Survive

Idioms about bodily sensations continue to thrive because they offer emotional, social and cognitive value. They survive across centuries for reasons that remain largely unchanged. These beliefs help people manage uncertainty, organise difficult emotions and maintain cultural continuity. They appear simple, yet each one carries a long history of psychological and social function. Frazer explains that cultural beliefs endure when they help people navigate fear, confusion or instability. Kahneman shows that humans favour simple explanations when they feel overwhelmed. These two forces keep bodily idioms alive even in societies that understand modern physiology.

Humans want answers. They want clarity. They want a sense of control when their bodies behave in unexpected ways. A warm ear, a tight chest or a twitching eye disrupts internal equilibrium. Idioms step in because they reduce tension. They give the sensation a place to sit. These beliefs remain persuasive because they were learned early and repeated often. They also survive because they work at a psychological level, even if they fail at a scientific one.

This chapter expands on the many factors that protect these beliefs from fading. Each factor plays a role. Together they create a system that keeps bodily idioms alive even in advanced societies.

EMOTIONAL SIMPLICITY

People prefer explanations that feel easy to understand. When a sudden sensation appears, the mind does not want a complex analysis. It wants quick closure. It wants to remove the uncertainty at once. Bodily idioms offer this closure. They give a short, repeatable explanation that ends the search for meaning.

A person who feels heat in one ear could evaluate temperature, circulation, stress, posture, hydration, caffeine intake or hormonal shifts. The average person will not do this. They will choose the simplest explanation. They will default to familiar cultural knowledge.

Kahneman explains this behaviour through fast thinking. Fast thinking handles uncertainty by using shortcuts. It selects explanations already stored in memory. These explanations do not need to be accurate. They only need to feel satisfying. When someone says their ear warmed because someone mentioned them, they use a familiar rule. The rule fills the gap. The discomfort decreases. The belief strengthens.

Emotional simplicity protects the idiom because it works in real time. It helps people feel calm when their bodies produce unexpected signals. People return to the idiom again and again because each use produces the same emotional effect. It becomes a habit. Habits are difficult to break.

This habit deepens when stress rises. Sapolsky shows that stress reduces analytical capacity. When stressed, people rely more on instinct. They accept simple explanations even when logic would reveal alternatives. A stressed person does not evaluate biology. They choose the idiom. The idiom feels right because it ends the discomfort.

CULTURAL CONTINUITY

Idioms survive through family lines and cultural transmission. People learn them before they understand physiology. Children hear adults repeat these sayings during everyday situations. When a child hears their grandmother say that a warm ear means someone mentioned them, they internalise it without questioning. The child accepts the rule because they trust the adult. The rule becomes part of the child's cultural vocabulary.

Frazer documents this style of transmission across continents. He shows that beliefs about bodily sensations appear consistently across generations because they become part of identity. People repeat them during childhood, adolescence and adulthood. They remain stable because they represent familiarity and continuity.

Cultural continuity gives idioms emotional weight. Adults use them not only to explain sensations but also to maintain connection with their heritage. The idiom becomes tied to memories of family conversations, childhood guidance or cultural rituals. The meaning shifts from literal interpretation to symbolic continuity. The belief stays because it feels woven into the family structure.

These sayings also survive transitions. When people migrate, they carry idioms into new environments. The idioms become even more significant because they preserve identity. They protect cultural memory in unfamiliar surroundings. They remind people of home and tradition. New generations adopt them because they offer comfort.

THE SOCIAL FUNCTION OF IDIOMS

Idioms help people communicate feelings that may be difficult to express directly. People often experience social uncertainty but hesitate to admit it. They may not want to say they feel watched, judged or dismissed. Instead, they use an idiom. The idiom expresses the feeling without exposing vulnerability.

Someone may say that their ear feels hot rather than admitting they feel insecure. The idiom becomes a socially safe tool. It communicates discomfort without demanding a personal disclosure. Dunbar notes that social groups rely on easy communication tools to navigate tension. Idioms offer this convenience.

Idioms also help people explore social meaning together. When two people share the same idiom, they understand each other quickly. They do not need long explanations. The idiom carries cultural context. It moves the conversation forward. This shared understanding protects social bonds. It creates a sense of unity. These benefits help idioms survive even when the original meaning becomes less relevant.

SOCIAL REHEARSAL AND GROUP BELONGING

Idioms act as a form of social rehearsal. People repeat them to practice navigating social meaning. Children use them to test emotional interpretations. Adults use them to interpret uncertain moments. The repetition strengthens group belonging. It reinforces social scripts.

When someone uses a common idiom, they show that they understand the cultural system. They demonstrate social awareness. This strengthens group identity. People continue to use idioms because they support belonging, not because they believe the literal meaning.

THE ROLE OF MEMORY

Beliefs about bodily sensations strengthen through selective memory. People remember the moments that appear to confirm the idiom. They forget the moments that contradict it. This pattern creates the illusion that the idiom works.

For example, someone feels heat in their ear during a conversation. They later hear that their name came up in a different context. The two events appear linked. The mind stores the link as confirmation. The belief gains power.

When someone feels heat in their ear yet nothing happens, they rarely remember it. The event has no emotional impact. Kahneman and Ariely explain that humans remember emotionally charged events more vividly than neutral ones. Confirmation creates emotional intensity. Neutral moments disappear.

This selective memory creates a skewed record. The belief appears consistent even though most sensations had no meaning. Over time, the belief solidifies.

This process becomes even stronger when people share stories within families. Relatives may recall a coincidental event that seemed to confirm the idiom. The story gains weight because it is repeated. It becomes part of family lore. These stories keep the belief alive long after its original purpose fades.

THE COMFORT OF SYMBOLIC THINKING

Symbolic thinking helps people organise internal experiences. Humans use symbols to understand feelings, relationships and uncertainty. Bodily sensations become symbols because they appear vivid. They interrupt daily life. They demand attention. People respond by assigning meaning that feels emotionally useful.

Frazer explains that symbolic thinking once helped communities understand environmental events. It now helps people understand internal events. A warm ear becomes a symbol for attention. A twitching limb becomes a symbol for news. A surge of heat becomes a symbol for emotional significance.

Symbolic thinking offers structure. It gives sensations an identity. It helps people feel that their experiences fit into a larger system. Radford notes that beliefs survive when they offer structure in moments of emotional ambiguity. Bodily idioms fit this rule perfectly.

When someone uses symbolic interpretation, they avoid the discomfort of uncertainty. The symbol carries enough meaning to close the gap. This psychological relief keeps the idiom alive.

BODILY UNCERTAINTY

Human bodies behave in ways that feel unpredictable. Unlike external events, internal signals often appear without context. People cannot see the cause of their sensations. They only feel them.

Craig explains that interoception captures internal signals that the brain struggles to interpret. These signals include temperature changes, tension, digestive movement, hormonal shifts and variations in circulation. The signals appear fast. They often feel intrusive. They feel personal because they arise from inside the body.

The mind dislikes unexplained sensations. Humans want to understand what happens inside their own bodies. When they cannot find clarity, they invent meaning. Idioms provide accessible explanations. They reduce the sense of randomness. They convert internal noise into a readable message.

This process runs automatically. The person does not choose it. The body reacts. The mind interprets. The idiom becomes a shortcut.

UNCERTAINTY AND SOCIAL THREAT

Social threat increases the need for fast explanations. When people feel insecure, uncertain or unnoticed, they rely on bodily idioms more heavily. The body becomes a source of perceived messages.

If someone fears being judged, they interpret a sensation as a sign of judgement. If someone fears exclusion, they interpret a sensation as a sign of social shift. Dunbar explains that humans evolved to detect social threat quickly because exclusion carried physical risk. This instinct remains active.

These interpretations feel logical in the moment even though they rest on assumption. The idiom functions as a bridge between sensation and fear. It allows the person to assign meaning without facing the full complexity of the emotional concern.

TRAUMA AND ATTACHMENT

People with trauma histories often rely more on bodily idioms because their nervous systems react strongly to uncertainty. Van der Kolk shows that trauma increases sensitivity to internal signals. These individuals experience stronger sensations, faster reactions and greater emotional intensity. They search for meaning in these signals because they feel overwhelming.

Attachment patterns amplify this behaviour. People with anxious attachment expect rejection. They interpret sensations through this expectation. They use bodily idioms to confirm fears, even when no evidence exists. The idiom becomes a tool that supports their emotional model.

These patterns help explain why bodily idioms remain persuasive across personality differences and life experiences. They serve different needs for different people. They remain flexible enough to apply broadly.

LINGUISTIC ENDURANCE

Language plays a major role in the survival of these beliefs. Once an idiom becomes embedded in a language, it becomes a cognitive tool. People use it automatically because it sits inside familiar speech. It becomes part of how people think.

Removing idioms from language is extremely difficult. Removing the meaning attached to an idiom is even harder. People use these sayings without considering whether they believe them. The idiom becomes a habit of expression. The habit reinforces the belief.

The linguist hears the idiom first. The emotional brain hears it second. Both influence behaviour.

WHY THE IDIOMS FEEL TRUE

These beliefs survive because they match emotional experience. They feel accurate. They feel intuitive. They feel socially logical. Kahneman explains that humans accept explanations that maintain coherence. Bodily idioms maintain coherence because they match the context in which they appear.

When someone feels heat during a tense moment, the idiom fits the emotion. When someone feels tension during uncertainty, the idiom fits the fear. When someone feels pressure during social stress, the idiom fits the worry. These matches strengthen the belief even when the biology tells a different story.

Bodily idioms survive because they offer psychological comfort, emotional clarity, social cohesion, cultural continuity and cognitive simplicity. They help people feel grounded when sensations appear without warning. They help communities maintain connection. They help individuals manage fear and uncertainty.

These beliefs endure even when scientific explanations exist because they solve problems that science does not address. They reduce emotional discomfort. They preserve cultural identity. They allow people to understand themselves when their bodies shift in unpredictable ways.

The next chapter shows how three people interpret the same sensation differently based on their cultural background. These stories demonstrate how environment shapes meaning even when the biology remains consistent.

17

Three People, Same Sensation, Different Worlds

Humans experience the same biological sensations, yet interpret them through entirely different cultural, personal and emotional lenses. A warm ear, a surge of tension or a shift in breathing can feel universal at the biological level. The physiology does not change from one community to another. Blood flow increases. Nerve activity shifts. Temperature rises. The brain tracks these changes through interoception. Craig explains that interoception works the same across cultures because it reflects shared human anatomy.

Despite this shared biology, interpretation varies widely. People attach meanings that reflect their upbringing, cultural expectations and social environment. Radford documents how communities convert the same bodily sensations into different signs. Frazer shows that symbolic beliefs emerge from local stories rather than universal facts. This chapter explores that pattern through three people who experience the identical sensation of ear warmth. Each person interprets the sensation in a way shaped by their cultural learning and emotional history.

THE NIGERIAN WOMAN: SPIRITUAL SIGNIFICANCE AND SOCIAL VISIBILITY

A woman in her early thirties prepares food in her family kitchen in Lagos. She feels a sudden heat in her right ear. The sensation appears fast. It interrupts her focus. She pauses because she grew up in a household where bodily sensations carried meaning. Her grandmother told her that right ear warmth means someone thinks well of you. Left ear warmth means someone speaks critically. These explanations formed early. They stayed with her because her family repeated them often.

In her community, the body sits inside a system of social and spiritual meaning. Yoruba and Igbo traditions treat sensations as signs. People assume that ancestors, family or community members may influence the moment. These explanations reduce uncertainty. They help people feel connected to others. The woman interprets the heat as a sign of positive mention. She feels encouraged by the idea. The belief matches her emotional state because she values connection with her extended family. She feels comforted knowing that someone may be speaking about her in a supportive way.

Van der Kolk notes that people who feel secure in their relationships often interpret sensations through the lens of connection rather than threat. This woman grew up with strong family ties. She trusts the cultural script. She accepts the meaning without conflict. The sensation becomes a sign of inclusion.

She continues preparing the meal with a sense of quiet assurance. The sensation stops. The interpretation remains. The belief feels valid because it aligns with her cultural expectations. She does not question it because she does not need to. It provides emotional value. It fits the meaning system around her. It reinforces her sense of belonging. The biology produced a standard response. Her mind produced a culturally shaped narrative.

THE ITALIAN MAN: GOSSIP, SOCIAL DYNAMICS AND COMMUNITY MEMORY

A middle aged man walks through a narrow street in a town outside Naples. He carries groceries from the market. The afternoon is warm, but the heat in his left ear feels sharper than the temperature around him. The sensation stands out. He learned from childhood that ear warmth can signal gossip. Italian communities hold strong traditions that connect bodily sensations with social meaning. He grew up hearing relatives say that the left ear means criticism. The right ear means praise. The belief survives because families repeat it. It became part of local humour and everyday talk.

The man values his reputation in the community. He knows many people. He talks to them often. He also knows that conversations about others happen frequently in small towns. Dunbar explains that gossip allows communities to monitor behaviour. It helps people understand their social position. The man expects gossip. He treats it as normal. When his ear warms, he assumes someone has discussed him. His mind moves fast. He thinks of recent interactions. He remembers a disagreement at work. He interprets the sensation as a sign that someone continued the conversation without him present.

His interpretation reflects cultural training. It also reflects his current concerns. He wants to protect his reputation. He wants to stay respected in his social circle. Kahneman explains that people interpret ambiguous information through their current emotional context. The man's context includes social vigilance. He attaches the meaning that feels most plausible to him.

The sensation fades within seconds, yet it leaves behind a narrative. He wonders which colleague might have raised his name. He debates whether the conversation involved criticism or misunderstanding. His cultural script supports this debate. It gives him tools to make sense of uncertainty. The belief does not cause him distress. It provides structure. It helps him release tension by assuming the explanation aligns with tradition. He continues walking. He accepts the interpretation because it fits his social environment.

THE INDIAN TEEN: COSMIC ORDER, ASTROLOGICAL STRUCTURE AND PERSONAL UNCERTAINTY

A sixteen year old student in Delhi studies for an exam. He feels sudden heat inside his left ear. He stops writing. The sensation feels strange because he is already stressed about the exam. Stress heightens interoceptive sensitivity. Critchley notes that anxious individuals detect internal shifts more intensely. The teen interprets the sensation through the framework he grew up with. His family follows traditional astrological beliefs. They treat bodily sensations as signs influenced by planetary positions.

He learned that certain twitches or temperature changes can correspond to favourable or unfavourable events. His parents sometimes consult astrological calendars before important decisions. He absorbed these practices throughout childhood. He now uses them to make sense of unfamiliar sensations.

When his ear warms, he interprets it as a possible omen. He does not think someone is speaking about him. Instead, he assumes the sensation relates to timing or fate. The belief system he grew up with links bodily shifts to cosmic order. He checks the clock. He wonders whether the sensation matches something he heard earlier about uncomfortable signs in the afternoon.

Ariely explains that when people feel uncertainty, they turn to structured beliefs that reduce cognitive load. Astrology provides structure. It gives meaning to the unknown. It makes randomness feel organised. The teen interprets the sensation through this structured system. He believes it may reflect emotional strain or upcoming challenges.

The sensation ends, but he continues thinking about its meaning. He wonders whether the sensation confirms his anxiety about the exam. He decides to take a short break because the interpretation gives him a reason to pause. The belief provides emotional relief. It helps him slow down. It fits the cultural and familial framework that shapes his thinking.

SHARED BIOLOGY, DIFFERENT STORIES

All three people experienced the same biological event. Blood flow changed. Temperature rose. Interoceptive signals reached their awareness. Craig's work explains that the sensation follows predictable physiological rules. Nothing about the biology differed across the three individuals. The difference emerged in interpretation.

The Nigerian woman interpreted the sensation through the lens of spiritual and social connection. The Italian man viewed it through the lens of gossip and community attention. The Indian teen viewed it through the lens of astrological structure and emotional uncertainty.

Each person responded to their cultural script. They accepted explanations learned early in life. They used these explanations to organise their emotional state. Frazer shows that cultural stories survive because they work. They help people feel anchored.

These interpretations matched their needs. The Nigerian woman needed connection. The Italian man needed clarity about reputation. The Indian teen needed a sense of order during stress. Their interpretations came from emotional relevance, not biological fact.

PERSONAL HISTORY AND CURRENT STRESS

Cultural meaning does not appear alone. It merges with personal memory and emotional context. Each person reacted through a lens shaped by past experiences. The Nigerian woman remembered her grandmother's guidance. The Italian man remembered past conflicts. The Indian teen felt exam pressure.

These personal layers shaped their interpretations as much as culture did.

Van der Kolk describes how memory influences physiological interpretation. People respond not only to current events but also to signals stored in their history. A familiar sensation triggers familiar explanations. This occurs without conscious thought.

People rarely examine these explanations. They feel natural because they were learned early. When learned early, beliefs about bodily sensations feel automatic. They attach themselves to identity. They provide stability when the body creates uncertainty.

SOCIAL CONTEXT AND MEANING

Each person's environment further shaped the meaning they created. The Nigerian woman lived in a community that valued spiritual continuity. Her explanation fit the environment. The Italian man lived in a tightly connected town where gossip carried real weight. His explanation matched the social setting. The Indian teen lived inside a family that used astrology in daily decisions. His explanation aligned with the family system.

Dunbar shows that humans adapt their interpretive habits to their social environment. The environment reinforces certain beliefs because they make sense inside that context. Each person felt that their interpretation was the most logical one available. They did not consider alternatives because the cultural explanation provided emotional comfort.

WHY THESE DIFFERENCES MATTER

These three stories show how easily humans personalise sensations. They also show how meaning depends on cultural structure. People believe their interpretation because it fits the social world they grew up in. It fits the emotional needs they carry. It fits the language they use to understand themselves.

The biology stays constant. The story changes. This pattern explains why bodily idioms thrive across continents. They offer meaning tailored to local expectations. They survive because they fulfil cultural roles that science cannot replace.

Humans do not interpret the body in isolation. They interpret the body through history, community, fear, hope and identity. They attach meaning that serves psychological needs. They fit sensations into stories that reflect who they are and where they live.

These three individuals show how the same sensation produces three different narratives. Their interpretations reflect their cultural upbringing, emotional context and personal concerns. Their beliefs reveal the persistence of symbolic thinking across societies. They also show the crucial role of culture in shaping how people understand their bodies.

The next chapter explains how the digital environment reshapes these ancient instincts. It shows how constant notifications, online visibility and digital comparison produce new versions of old fears. The same biology reacts inside a modern world filled with continuous social cues.

PART VI

MODERN PSYCHOLOGY, ANCIENT INSTINCTS

18

The Burn of the Digital Age

Humans now live inside a world that exposes them to more signals, more opinions and more social visibility than any previous generation. The digital environment changed how people interpret attention. It also changed how they react to ordinary sensations. What once felt like a small moment can now feel loaded. What once felt private now carries the risk of public reaction. The body reacts fast because the stakes feel higher. The mind follows with assumptions shaped by constant comparison, fear of missing out and the need to stay visible.

This chapter explains why digital life makes people misinterpret sensations more often. It also shows how online environments amplify fear of judgement. These changes occur because the brain treats digital cues as social events. A notification, unread message or paused reply can activate the same circuits that once responded to threats in small communities. Turkle's research outlines how digital interactions mimic the intensity of real social encounters. The body reacts before the person can apply logic. The reaction often feels personal.

Jason A. Solomon, B.Ed

PHANTOM SIGNALS FROM A HYPERCONNECTED WORLD

Many people feel vibrations that never occurred. They feel the phone buzz even when it stayed still. They sense heat in their ears after reading a vague message. They feel a shift in their chest while waiting for a response. These sensations appear because the brain has adapted to constant alerts. When alerts stop, the body fills the silence with expectation. This expectation creates phantom sensations.

This phenomenon develops because the brain learns patterns quickly. When a person receives many messages each day, their body prepares for the next one. Muscles tense. Breathing changes. Heat shifts across the skin. People misread these sensations because they expect something to happen. The mind wants confirmation. Kahneman explains that humans interpret new sensations through the lens of expectation. The expectation shapes the story. The story feels convincing.

Digital alerts activate the social alarm system. Each message or comment feels like a cue that someone has judged you, noticed you or ignored you. Your nervous system responds with speed. A warm ear may appear at the same moment you receive a notification. The timing feels meaningful even though the sensation formed from biology.

THE BODY TREATS DIGITAL ATTENTION AS REAL ATTENTION

Humans evolved inside groups where every social cue mattered. Approval provided safety. Rejection increased danger. The brain has not changed. It still treats each sign of attention as important. A message, comment or reaction can trigger the same circuits that once responded to physical proximity. The body cannot tell the difference between an online cue and an in person cue.

Turkle highlights this issue in her work. She found that people experience digital interactions with emotional intensity equal to face to face contact. A vague message can trigger physical tension. A delayed reply can activate the same circuits that respond to rejection. The physical sensation comes first. The interpretation comes next. The interpretation forms from fear of losing connection.

This environment increases curiosity. People want to know who reacted. They want to know what others think. They want to know why someone clicked on their profile. Curiosity becomes a daily behaviour. It merges with a Fear of Missing Out (FOMO). People expect to miss something if they do not monitor their digital world. The expectation increases stress. Stress amplifies interoceptive signals. The person notices every warm ear, every shift in breathing, every pulse of tension.

FOMO AND THE DRIVE TO STAY UPDATED

Fear of missing out changes how people respond to normal sensations. When someone expects new information at any moment, their body stays alert. This alertness raises arousal levels. Higher arousal produces more internal noise. The person feels more sensations. They interpret the sensations as meaningful.

Someone checks their phone often because they fear missing a message. If they feel warmth in their ear, they assume it relates to a change in their social world. The sensation becomes a cue. The cue produces urgency. The urgency fuels more checking. The cycle continues. Ariely describes this pattern as a desire for quick reassurance. People want to confirm that they remain included. They want to confirm that nothing important occurred without them. FOMO increases the emotional weight of minor shifts in the body.

The digital environment feeds this cycle with constant comparison. People see others receive attention. They see others gain approval. They fear falling behind. This fear makes them monitor their own social signals. Any sensation feels like evidence of change. They worry the moment they feel heat. They wonder whether someone mentioned them. The body becomes a source of suspicion.

THE PRESSURE OF CONSTANT VISIBILITY

People now live in a world where anyone can observe them at any time. Online presence creates a form of public exposure that previous generations did not face. Every message, photo or comment can be evaluated. People internalise this exposure. The mind becomes hyperaware of judgement. The body reacts to this awareness before the mind identifies a trigger.

A person may feel heat in their ear after posting something online. They assume someone reacted negatively. They expect criticism because digital environments teach people to anticipate it. They know that silence online can feel like rejection. They know that small shifts in behaviour can signal disinterest. Their body prepares for judgement. The sensation becomes part of a social narrative.

Dunbar's work shows that humans monitor their social position continuously. The digital world expands this instinct. People track more relationships than their brains can manage. Dunbar found that humans can maintain stable social awareness for about one hundred and fifty connections. Modern platforms expose people to hundreds or thousands of individuals. The brain struggles to track them. The struggle increases anxiety. Anxiety makes sensations feel sharper.

THE DOPAMINE LOOP OF NOTIFICATIONS

Notifications reward attention. They release dopamine. This chemical reinforces checking behaviour. The more someone checks, the more they expect new signals. The expectation increases arousal. Arousal increases internal sensations. People feel tension or heat because their body sits in a constant state of anticipation.

When notification patterns shift, the person notices immediately. If they usually receive many messages but experience a sudden pause, they treat the pause as meaningful. Their ear warms. Their chest tightens. Their mind links the sensation to the silence. The silence feels social. The sensation feels like proof.

Turkle notes that people now treat their digital presence as part of their identity. They interpret bodily sensations through this identity. They ask whether the sensation reflects visibility, status or relevance. They ask whether people still care. They ask whether they missed something important. FOMO shapes every interpretation.

HOW DIGITAL CUES CREATE FALSE ALARMS

Digital interactions contain many ambiguous signals. A message read but not answered. A post viewed but not acknowledged. A comment typed but deleted. A brief pause in conversation. People fill these gaps with assumptions because gaps create discomfort. The discomfort produces bodily signals. The signals feel personal. The person misinterprets the signals as evidence.

Kahneman explains that the mind dislikes incomplete information. It fills gaps with stories. These stories align with internal fears. Someone who fears rejection interprets silence as rejection. Someone who fears exclusion interprets pauses as exclusion. A warm ear during these moments gains emotional weight.

People now face more ambiguous cues than ever before. Digital communication lacks tone, posture and facial expression. The brain wants clarity. The body reacts when clarity does not arrive. Internal sensations intensify. Interpretation follows.

HOW THE DIGITAL AGE REINFORCES ANCIENT INSTINCTS

Online environments do not create new psychology. They amplify old instincts. Humans evolved to monitor gossip and reputation. They evolved to detect threat. They evolved to track alliances and status. The digital world increases exposure to these cues. It makes them constant. It makes them immediate. It makes them unavoidable.

The gap between sensation and meaning grows smaller because digital interactions create emotional urgency. People want to stay updated. They want to remain relevant. They want to avoid missing something that might affect their social position. FOMO magnifies every signal. Curiosity makes every sensation feel like a clue.

This environment pushes people to interpret their bodies through fear and anticipation. A warm ear becomes a sign of new information. A shift in breathing becomes a sign of social change. A moment of tension becomes a sign of conflict. The sensation carries emotional urgency because the person fears missing something important.

The digital age intensifies how humans interpret bodily sensations. It increases curiosity. It amplifies FOMO. It creates more reasons to question whether others have mentioned you. It adds more uncertainty to the social world. It makes internal sensations feel linked to external events.

People now live in a constant cycle of anticipation. The body reacts first. The mind tries to keep up. The interpretation often reflects digital habits more than real events.

The next chapter explains why anxiety forms loops in these situations. It shows how sensations, thoughts and assumptions reinforce each other until the story feels undeniable. You will see why the body keeps reacting even when the environment stays safe.

19

The Anxiety Loop

Anxiety forms patterns. It does not appear in random bursts. It builds from small triggers, grows through assumptions and settles into habits that feel automatic. The body reacts first. The mind explains the reaction. The explanation shapes the next reaction. The cycle continues until the person cannot tell the difference between sensation and meaning. This loop shapes how people interpret heat, tension, tingling and pressure. It affects how they respond to digital cues, social uncertainty and sudden body signals. Kahneman notes that humans rely on fast thinking when stressed. Fast thinking accepts the first explanation available. Anxiety strengthens this tendency.

This chapter explores how the loop forms, why it repeats and how it takes control of everyday life. It also shows how trauma, attachment history and fear of rejection intensify the cycle. People rarely recognise the loop while they are inside it. They feel the symptoms but miss the pattern. Understanding the pattern brings the first step toward breaking it.

THE FIRST STEP: SENSATION

The loop begins with a sensation. The sensation may be mild. It may be a warm ear, a tight chest, a rising pulse or a brief tension in the stomach. These sensations form from biology. They appear because the body regulates temperature, circulation, hormones or stress responses. Craig's work on interoception shows that people notice sensations more when anxious, tired or overwhelmed.

The sensation feels personal because it comes from inside the body. The person pays attention to it. They try to understand it. The search for meaning begins at once. Anxiety acts as a filter. It highlights the sensation with intensity. It makes the sensation feel important. The body sets the stage before the mind steps in.

THE SECOND STEP: THOUGHT

Humans explain sensations through thought. The mind interprets before it checks facts. The interpretation reflects emotional state more than objective conditions. When someone feels anxious, they interpret signals through fear. They ask the wrong questions. They ask what the sensation means rather than what caused it.

An anxious person might think:

- Why did this happen
- Who is talking about me
- Did I upset someone
- Did I miss something

Is this a sign of danger

These thoughts form quickly. Kahneman explains that the brain seeks coherence, not accuracy. The brain wants a story that explains the discomfort. The story appears instantly. It feels convincing because it reduces uncertainty. Ariely notes that humans accept simple, immediate explanations when stressed because the alternatives feel overwhelming.

The person does not question these interpretations. They accept them because they match the emotional tone of the moment.

THE THIRD STEP: EMOTION

Once the thought forms, emotion develops. The emotion reflects the interpretation. If the person believes the sensation signals danger, they feel fear. If they believe it signals judgement, they feel shame. If they believe it signals conflict, they feel threat. The emotion strengthens the interpretation even when the interpretation has no evidence.

Emotion increases physical arousal. The heart rate rises. Muscles tense. Heat spreads through the body. These reactions create new sensations. The sensations confirm the story. The person misreads the biological response as proof. This creates the next layer of the loop.

THE FOURTH STEP: CONFIRMATION

Confirmation forms when the mind links emotion with sensation. The person feels tense because they believed the sensation carried meaning. The tension feels like evidence. They interpret the tension as further proof that something is wrong.

The cycle now reinforces itself. The person believes their interpretation. The belief shapes the next wave of sensations. The sensations amplify the fear. The fear strengthens the interpretation. This loop continues until the person becomes convinced that the sensation reflects real danger.

Kahneman calls this pattern a coherence error. The mind makes a full story from partial signals. The story feels complete even when the signals came from biology rather than external events.

THE FIFTH STEP: BEHAVIOUR

The person changes behaviour because of the belief. They may check their phone repeatedly. They may review conversations in their mind. They may avoid certain people. They may withdraw from social situations. They may overthink every interaction. Their behaviour shifts because the belief feels real.

These behavioural changes increase anxiety. Avoidance reduces confidence. Overchecking increases uncertainty. Excessive reflection increases stress. Each behaviour feeds the loop.

Dunbar notes that humans react strongly to perceived social threat. When behaviour reflects fear of rejection, the brain treats the situation as serious. The body stays alert. It continues to produce sensations. The loop deepens.

THE LOOP RESTARTS

After the behaviour changes, a new sensation appears. The sensation may be minor. It might be a warm ear again. It might be a flutter in the chest. It might be pressure in the shoulders. The person notices it because anxiety increases sensitivity. They interpret it through fear. The cycle begins again.

This loop can run many times each day. It can run without the person noticing. It can run during small interactions, digital delays or moments of silence. It becomes a habit. Habits become automatic because the brain tries to conserve effort. The loop requires little conscious thought.

WHY THE LOOP IS STRONG

The anxiety loop remains strong because each step feels logical inside the moment. The person feels a sensation. They attach meaning. They react emotionally. The emotion strengthens the meaning. The physical reinforcement makes the belief feel credible. The next sensation arrives. The loop deepens. It becomes self-sustaining.

Humans trust internal signals because internal signals feel intimate. They feel personal. They feel accurate. Craig explains that interoceptive signals gain emotional weight because they originate inside the body. People assume internal messages reflect truth even when they reflect biology.

Fear strengthens this trust. When afraid, humans rely less on reasoning and more on instinct. Instinct focuses on survival. Instinct does not question interpretations. It acts immediately. Sapolsky notes that stress reduces cognitive flexibility. The person becomes less capable of evaluating alternative explanations.

TRAUMA INTENSIFIES THE LOOP

Trauma increases sensitivity to sensations. Van der Kolk shows that trauma changes how the nervous system responds. The system reacts faster and stronger. The person notices more internal activity. They interpret these signals through past experiences. They assume danger even when safe.

A warm ear may feel harmless in a calm person. In someone with trauma, it may feel like a warning. Trauma stores memory in the body. The sensation triggers old fear. The old fear shapes new interpretation. This makes the loop stronger and harder to break.

ATTACHMENT SHAPES INTERPRETATION

Attachment history influences how someone interprets sensations. People with anxious attachment expect rejection. They interpret neutral cues as negative. They assume others judge them. When they feel heat or tension, they treat the sensation as proof that rejection occurred.

People with avoidant attachment may disconnect from sensations, yet react strongly to social threat. They may feel a sudden shift in their body and assume they must withdraw. The loop forms even if they refuse to acknowledge their fear.

Attachment does not control biology. It controls interpretation. Interpretation controls emotion. Emotion controls the loop.

THE ROLE OF DIGITAL HABITS

Digital habits strengthen the loop by amplifying uncertainty. People expect constant updates. They expect instant replies. They expect clear signals. When these expectations fail, they enter uncertainty. Uncertainty activates the loop.

The body reacts to digital silence. A sensation appears. The mind fills the silence with meaning. The meaning aligns with fear. The cycle strengthens. Turkle notes that digital environments reward vigilance. They turn checking into a habit. The habit increases anxiety. Anxiety increases the intensity of sensations.

Many people misinterpret digital cues because they cannot see the full context. They rely on internal sensations instead of external information. This accelerates the loop.

WHY THE LOOP FEELS TRUE

The loop feels accurate because it uses the body as evidence. Humans trust bodily signals even when the signals come from stress or hormones. The loop produces sensations that feel convincing. The mind misreads the sensations as confirmation of the belief. The belief becomes stronger. The loop becomes harder to break.

The loop also fits emotional expectations. People often interpret sensations in ways that match their fears. If someone fears being ignored, they interpret a sensation as proof of disinterest. If someone fears conflict, they interpret it as evidence of tension. Kahneman notes that humans build stories that fit their emotional state. The loop exploits this habit.

WHEN THE LOOP TAKES OVER DAILY LIFE

Inside the loop, every sensation becomes a possible threat. Every shift in temperature feels meaningful. Every moment of tension feels like a message. The person monitors themselves constantly. This monitoring increases anxiety. Anxiety increases sensitivity. Sensitivity increases misinterpretation.

People trapped in the loop often feel exhausted. They spend energy evaluating sensations. They rehearse conversations. They anticipate criticism. They fear social mistakes. The loop becomes a background process that drains emotional resources.

HOW THE LOOP BREAKS

Breaking the loop requires awareness. The person must see the pattern. They must notice that the sensation came first. They must recognise that the thought appeared because of fear, not evidence. They must identify the moment when emotion shaped interpretation. The loop weakens when the person questions the story.

They also must understand that sensations reflect biology. Craig and Critchley show that interoception becomes louder when someone is anxious, stressed or overwhelmed. When the person learns to identify these conditions, they can detach sensation from meaning.

Awareness disrupts the cycle. It does not remove sensations. It changes their interpretation. Interpretation controls emotion. Once emotion reduces, the loop loses power.

The anxiety loop explains why people misinterpret internal signals. It shows how body, thought, emotion and behaviour reinforce each other. It reveals why sensations feel meaningful even when they are not. It explains why people continue to believe stories that began with biology rather than reality.

This loop affects anyone who faces stress, uncertainty, rejection sensitivity or digital overload. It becomes stronger when people feel vulnerable. It becomes weaker when they learn to separate sensation from interpretation.

The next chapter shows how to rewrite the internal story. It provides tools that help people recognise accuracy, challenge interpretations and build a healthier relationship with bodily signals.

20

Rewriting the Story

Humans feel bodily sensations before they form conscious interpretations. Heat, pressure, tension and tingling arrive fast. The mind responds with explanations that fit emotional habits. These explanations feel natural, yet many come from fear, stress or old narratives. Kahneman shows that fast thinking creates confident stories even when evidence is missing. These stories shape identity and behaviour. They shape how people respond to uncertainty, conflict and social pressure.

Rewriting the story does not remove sensations. It changes how people understand them. It creates space between biology and belief. It helps people recognise when their mind builds a narrative from fear rather than fact. This chapter offers tools based on modern science. It introduces strategies from Damasio, Craig, Sapolsky and de Becker. It also explores why people struggle to trust intuition when anxiety distorts their interpretation. Each section aims to build curiosity in the reader. It invites you to examine your own patterns. It highlights the risk of ignoring internal information for too long and shows why understanding your signals matters more than ever.

WHY REINTERPRETATION MATTERS

Humans live inside a world filled with constant evaluation. People observe each other online and offline. They scroll through profiles. They track reactions. They receive messages at unpredictable times. Every cue feels loaded. Every silence feels meaningful. People fear missing important information. They fear losing social relevance. They fear falling behind.

This environment increases the pressure to interpret sensations quickly. When someone feels heat in the ear or a rise in the chest, they assume it signals something urgent. They worry that the sensation warns them about a shift in their social world. They worry they missed a message or comment. They worry that someone judged them in silence.

Craig explains that interoceptive signals increase in intensity when stress rises. People misinterpret them because the signals feel significant. They want answers. They want clarity. They want reassurance. These desires shape interpretation.

Reinterpretation matters because the old explanations no longer protect people. They create unnecessary threat. They increase anxiety. They build assumptions that damage confidence. When someone learns to reinterpret sensations, they break the cycle. They gain control over patterns that once controlled them.

THE FIRST TOOL: ACCURATE INTEROCEPTION

Accurate interoception involves identifying a sensation without attaching meaning. It requires awareness of the physical event separate from emotional interpretation. Damasio shows that the brain builds emotional meaning from physiological signals. When someone learns to view the sensation as information, they reduce the emotional load.

To build accurate interoception, the person must ask:

- What do I feel
- Where do I feel it
- How strong is it
- How long does it last

These questions shift focus from story to observation. They interrupt the first impulse to assign meaning. The process increases clarity. It removes emotional fog. It helps the mind examine the signal without fear. Many people avoid these questions because they fear what the answers might reveal. This avoidance keeps the loop alive.

People who practise accurate interoception often notice something surprising. The sensation fades faster when they stop building a narrative around it. The narrative, not the sensation, created the emotional weight.

THE SECOND TOOL: COGNITIVE REFRAMING

Cognitive reframing challenges the interpretation that appears first. Kahneman notes that early interpretations come from fast thinking. Fast thinking favours familiar stories, not accurate ones. Reframing forces the mind to slow down. Slow thinking examines the story. It asks whether the interpretation fits the facts.

To reframe a sensation, the person must ask:

- What else could this mean
- What evidence supports my interpretation
- What evidence contradicts it
- Would I interpret this differently if I felt calm

These questions reveal how quickly the mind jumps to threat. They reveal how little evidence exists. They expose the emotional bias behind the story. When someone realises how fast the story formed, they gain distance from it.

This process increases curiosity. It pushes the person to explore their mind rather than fear it. It also reduces FOMO. When someone reframes the story, they learn that most sensations do not relate to missed information or hidden events. They relate to biology, stress or habit.

THE THIRD TOOL: REDUCING FALSE INTUITION

Many people confuse intuition with anxiety. Anxiety feels urgent. It feels strong. It feels meaningful. It creates a false sense of certainty. De Becker explains that true intuition comes from pattern recognition, not fear. Anxiety comes from internal noise. People who rely on anxious signals interpret sensations as warnings even when no threat exists.

To identify genuine intuition, the person must examine the conditions that produced the sensation. True intuition often follows exposure to small cues over time. It emerges from quiet recognition. Anxiety appears during stress, uncertainty or emotional pressure. It appears quickly. It feels forceful.

To reduce false intuition, the person must track:

- emotional triggers
- sleep quality
- stress levels
- digital exposure
- recent conflicts
- social uncertainty

These factors influence sensation. When someone recognises them, they learn to separate intuition from fear. This process builds confidence. It reduces the risk of misinterpreting signals. It prevents the person from acting on assumptions that damage relationships.

THE FOURTH TOOL: UNDERSTANDING THE STRESS RESPONSE

Sapolsky notes that stress changes the body in predictable ways. It increases heart rate. It raises temperature. It shifts blood flow. It activates muscle tension. These changes produce sensations that feel strong enough to create stories.

People misinterpret these sensations because they do not recognise the stress response. They treat the signals as personal messages rather than biological patterns. When they learn the mechanics of stress, they reduce the sense of alarm. They understand that a warm ear forms from circulation changes. They understand that tension in the chest comes from adrenaline. They understand that biological noise mimics emotional meaning.

Understanding stress removes the fear that builds the story.

THE FIFTH TOOL: REBUILDING TRUST WITH THE BODY

Many people distrust their bodily signals because they interpret them through anxiety. They fear sensations. They avoid them. They resist them. This resistance increases sensitivity. The more someone tries not to feel, the more they notice. The fear increases.

Rebuilding trust requires exposure. The person must let themselves feel sensations without reacting. They must sit with them. They must observe them. Over time, the sensations lose emotional power. The person begins to understand their patterns. They recognise that the body sends signals for many reasons unrelated to social events.

Rebuilding trust also reduces FOMO. People learn that sensations do not always relate to missed information. They relate to physical processes. When someone stops treating every sensation as a hint about their social world, they feel less pressure to monitor everything.

THE SIXTH TOOL: USING CURIOSITY TO REPLACE FEAR

Curiosity weakens anxiety because it changes the tone of interpretation. Fear demands certainty. Curiosity seeks information. Fear assumes threat. Curiosity explores possibilities. Fear closes the mind. Curiosity opens it.

Craig notes that people interpret interoceptive signals with far more clarity when they approach them with interest rather than threat. When someone becomes curious about their patterns, they stop treating sensations as warnings. They treat them as data.

Curiosity also reduces FOMO. When someone becomes curious, they stop assuming every sensation relates to social relevance. They start asking new questions. They want to understand their physiology. They want to investigate their biases. They want to examine their emotional habits.

This shift increases insight. It builds internal stability. It helps the person step out of the anxiety loop.

THE SEVENTH TOOL: LIMITING DIGITAL TRIGGERS

Digital environments produce many ambiguous cues. These cues activate the anxiety loop. They produce sensations that feel linked to social meaning. People cannot break the loop while they remain overloaded. They must reduce the triggers.

Limiting digital triggers does not require total withdrawal. It requires structured use. People benefit from:

- scheduled checking
- reduced notifications
- quiet periods
- boundaries around messaging
- removal of signals that create uncertainty

Turkle shows that constant monitoring increases anxiety. It also increases bodily sensitivity. When someone reduces digital noise, their nervous system steps out of hypervigilance. Their sensations become quieter. Their interpretations become clearer.

This process reduces FOMO because the person stops waiting for signals. They stop expecting constant updates. They reduce the pressure that drives misinterpretation.

WHY PEOPLE RESIST REINTERPRETATION

People resist reinterpretation because the old story feels familiar. It offers predictability even when it increases fear. Humans cling to familiar explanations. Kahneman notes that coherence feels safer than accuracy. The anxiety loop creates coherence. Reinterpretation disrupts the coherence. Disruption feels uncomfortable.

People also fear losing social awareness. They worry that ignoring sensations will cause them to miss important signals. They fear the cost of missing a threat. They fear the cost of missing information. They fear the cost of missing judgement. This fear creates resistance.

The truth is simple. People already miss signals when they rely on anxious interpretation. Anxiety narrows their view. It distorts social cues. It creates false alarms that drown out real intuition.

Reinterpretation increases accuracy. It sharpens awareness. It improves decision making.

REWRITING THE STORY IN REAL LIFE

Rewriting the story requires practice. It requires patience. It requires vulnerability. The person must face their fears. They must accept that many sensations reflect biology rather than social threat. They must learn to observe without reacting.

Over time, the new story becomes natural. The person begins to trust their body. They recognise patterns. They rely on curiosity instead of fear. They respond to real cues rather than imagined ones. They gain access to accurate intuition. They reduce FOMO because they no longer treat every signal as urgent.

The new story becomes a tool for clearer thinking, calmer interpretation and stronger emotional grounding.

Rewriting the story does not change the body. It changes the interpretation. It turns fear into awareness. It turns anxiety into observation. It turns false alarms into data. It creates space for clarity. It gives the person control over patterns that once controlled them.

This chapter brings the tools together to help you build a healthier relationship with your internal world. It sets the foundation for the final section of the book, where the focus shifts to long term stability. The next section explains how ancient instincts still guide modern behaviour and how you can work with them rather than fight them.

Conclusion

What Your Body Knows Before You Do

Your body signals before your mind forms meaning. This pattern shaped life in ancient communities and still shapes daily behaviour in modern societies. People notice heat, tension, tingling and pressure. They interpret these sensations immediately. The interpretations feel natural because they come from habits built over years. They come from cultural stories repeated across generations. They come from personal fears, past experiences and emotional expectations. These interpretations guide behaviour even when they form from assumptions rather than evidence.

Throughout this book, the pattern remained clear. A sensation arrives first. The mind responds with a story. The story influences emotion. Emotion strengthens the story. The loop continues until the sensation feels meaningful. Humans rely on these interpretations because the mind dislikes uncertainty. Kahneman explains that the brain seeks fast explanation. It wants coherence. It wants closure. It wants to know why the body shifted. This need for clarity drives people to interpret sensations as signs rather than biology.

The truth is simpler. Most sensations reflect physiology, not social threat. Craig shows that the body produces internal noise throughout the day. Blood flow changes. Hormones shift. Muscles contract. Temperature rises and falls. These shifts become louder during stress. They become sharper during uncertainty. They become more noticeable when someone feels watched or judged. The biology remains stable. The interpretation varies.

Humans attach meaning because meaning provides comfort. People want to know whether others talk about them. They want to understand where they stand in their social world. They fear missing important information. They fear losing relevance. They fear falling behind. This fear increases attention to bodily signals. It creates urgency. It fuels curiosity. It encourages people to treat each sensation as a clue. FOMO amplifies this tendency. People watch for signs that something changed without their knowledge. They monitor their internal world to predict their external one.

The stories from different cultures showed how strong these interpretations can become. A Nigerian woman felt warmth and thought of family connection. An Italian man felt warmth and assumed local gossip. An Indian teen felt warmth and connected it to cosmic timing. Their biology matched. Their interpretations did not. Frazer and Radford show that cultural stories survive because they help people organise emotion. These stories offer structure when the body feels unpredictable. They provide a sense of belonging when the mind feels uncertain.

Modern life increases the intensity of these responses. Digital platforms create constant exposure to judgement. People track likes, views, comments and messages. They expect feedback at all hours. Silence feels like rejection. Delay feels like criticism. Every interaction feels loaded. Turkle notes that digital cues activate the same circuits that respond to face to face evaluation. The body reacts with heat, tension and spikes of arousal. These reactions feel meaningful because the environment encourages vigilance.

This environment creates new forms of FOMO. People fear missing updates. They fear missing conversations. They fear losing connection. They fear that others moved ahead while they remained unaware. Each new notification strengthens the habit. Each pause in contact creates doubt. Doubt produces sensations. Sensations produce new interpretations. The loop continues.

Anxiety strengthens these patterns further. Sapolsky shows that stress changes physiology in predictable ways. When someone feels stressed, their nerves fire more often. Their circulation shifts. Their breathing tightens. These changes feel personal. They feel urgent. The person links them to social events even when no connection exists. The body reacts because it recognises strain. The mind reacts because it expects trouble.

Trauma intensifies the loop. Van der Kolk explains that trauma increases sensitivity to internal signals. People with trauma histories often interpret sensations through old memories. A warm ear becomes a warning. A tight chest becomes a sign of conflict. These interpretations feel accurate because they match emotional memory. Trauma shapes the way someone sees the world. It also shapes how they interpret their body.

Understanding this pattern does not remove vulnerability. It gives clarity. It shows why sensations feel significant even when they come from simple biological processes. It reveals how culture, memory and fear influence interpretation. It helps people question the stories that formed early in life.

Rewriting the internal story requires curiosity. Curiosity replaces fear with investigation. It encourages people to ask new questions. It invites them to explore rather than assume. Curiosity reduces the urgency that fuels FOMO. It slows the impulse to treat every sensation as a message about social relevance. It helps people observe their body without imagining hidden meaning.

When you learn to separate sensation from interpretation, the stories lose their weight. You see the process unfold. You recognise the moment the narrative begins. You understand why your mind linked the sensation to a social fear. You realise how fast the story formed. This awareness gives you space. It gives you control. It gives you accuracy.

Cognitive reframing strengthens this process. When you question your first interpretation, you force slow thinking to activate. Slow thinking checks the facts. It evaluates the emotional bias. It identifies alternative explanations. It exposes the habits that once felt automatic. Kahneman shows that slow thinking promotes accuracy. It challenges assumptions that fast thinking protects.

Accurate interoception builds trust in the body. When you observe sensations closely, you learn their patterns. You learn how they appear, how they shift and how they resolve. You discover that many sensations fade when you stop treating them as warnings. The fear dissolves. The biological rhythm returns. The body becomes less mysterious. It becomes familiar. Familiarity reduces anxiety.

Trust builds when you stop fighting your internal signals. Tension reduced through attention. Sensations lost power when you noticed them without panic. Curiosity replaced fear. The loop weakened. Biology became just biology.

Rewriting the story does not silence the body. It helps you listen more clearly. It teaches you to recognise which signals reflect fear and which reflect instinct. De Becker notes that true intuition comes from pattern recognition, not panic. When you learn to recognise your emotional triggers, your patterns of fear and the conditions that distort your thinking, you unlock genuine intuition. You gain the ability to interpret real cues rather than imagined ones.

This shift changes how you move through life. You stop assuming danger where none exists. You stop confusing stress for meaning. You stop attaching social narratives to biological events. You stop fearing sensations that form from fatigue or tension. You stop treating your body like an unreliable messenger.

You learn to recognise when your mind builds stories to fill gaps. You learn to identify the first moment the narrative appears. You learn to break the cycle before it becomes a loop. You learn to hold your interpretations lightly. You learn to trust your ability to analyse rather than react.

You also learn something important. The body whispers. It does not predict the future. It signals internal states, not external events. It reflects biology, not hidden conversations. It alerts you to strain, not gossip. These signals give you information that helps you understand yourself, not others. The interpretation belongs to you.

This book revealed why humans treat bodily sensations as messages. It explored old customs, ancient beliefs and cultural idioms. It examined the biology that created the sensations. It explained the psychology that shaped the stories. It showed how modern environments intensify old instincts. It revealed how anxiety forms loops that distort interpretation. It offered tools that help you rewrite the story.

The next step belongs to you. Your body will continue to send signals. Your mind will continue to search for meaning. You now understand where that meaning comes from. You know how to question it. You know how to recognise fear, habit, culture and stress. You know how to trace the story back to the moment the sensation appeared.

Your body knows things before you do. It always has. Now you know how to listen without assuming danger. Now you know how to observe without building stories that increase fear. Now you know how to interpret yourself with clarity instead of panic.

You can hear the signals. You can understand the patterns. You can trust your intuition without confusing it with anxiety.

The sensation comes first. The interpretation belongs to you.

COMPANION MATERIALS

Jason A. Solomon, B.Ed

WORKBOOK

Track Your Social Triggers

This workbook helps you map the link between body sensation, interpretation and behaviour. It gives you structure so you can see patterns that once felt random. Most people notice their triggers only after they react. This workbook helps you notice them earlier. It also helps you separate sensation from story so you can build accuracy instead of fear.

You can complete each section daily or whenever a strong sensation appears. The more often you record your reactions, the clearer your patterns become.

DAILY SENSATION LOG

Use this section to record what your body did before your mind reacted. Keep your responses brief. Focus on observation rather than meaning.

- Time of day
- Location
- People present
- Sensation felt
- Where in the body
- Intensity from one to ten
- Duration

This log helps you see when your body reacts most. Many people discover that certain times of day produce more tension. Others find that hunger, fatigue, digital overload or recent stress increase sensations. Craig's research shows that internal signals grow louder when the nervous system carries strain. Your log will reveal these patterns faster than memory.

TRIGGER TRACKING

This section helps you identify what happened just before the sensation. Do not guess. Record only what you noticed.

- Did someone speak
- Did someone pause
- Did someone look away
- Did someone whisper
- Did a message arrive
- Did a message fail to arrive
- Did the environment shift

When you track triggers, you learn how your mind links events to sensation. Many people discover that their triggers feel social but come from noise, temperature changes, digital cues or unrelated behaviour around them. This insight weakens old habits.

INTERPRETATION JOURNAL

Write the first thought that appeared when the sensation started. Keep it honest. Do not edit to sound calm. Anxiety reveals itself through the first interpretation, not the second or third.

- My first explanation was
- What I feared might be true
- What I assumed without evidence
- How strong the thought felt
- After recording the first explanation, add a second section.
- Facts that support my belief
- Facts that contradict it
- What else the sensation could mean

This step activates slow thinking. Kahneman shows that slow thinking helps people judge accuracy. When you force yourself to check the facts, the story becomes easier to challenge.

BODY AWARENESS EXERCISES

Use these exercises to strengthen accurate interoception. They help you notice what you feel without guessing why you feel it.

Sit for one minute. Notice one sensation in the body. Name the location. Rate the intensity. Describe how it shifts. Do not attach meaning.

Place your hand on your chest. Track your breathing for ten cycles. Record how your breathing changes.

Stand in a quiet room. Notice three sensations below the shoulders. Write each one without interpretation.

These drills train you to observe rather than assume. Damasio notes that emotional clarity increases when people understand their physical state. These exercises build that understanding.

SOCIAL ANXIETY MAPPING

Many people feel social pressure before they enter a room or read a message. This section helps you map the situations that produce tension.

Rate your anxiety in these environments from one to ten.

- Workplaces
- Family events
- Social media
- Friend groups
- Meetings
- Public speaking

- Dating
- Group discussions
- Messages or calls
- Silent rooms

After you complete the ratings, answer these questions.

- Where do I feel the most pressure
- Where do I expect judgement
- Where do I assume rejection
- Where do I overinterpret silence
- Where do I rely on guesswork instead of evidence

These reflections reveal how your environment shapes your internal world. Sapolsky notes that stress becomes predictable when you identify the situations that activate it. Mapping brings precision.

REFRAMING STRATEGIES

Use this section to interrupt the anxiety loop. These strategies help you step back before the story forms. Ask

- What else could this sensation be
- Would I think the same thing if I felt calm
- What evidence supports my explanation
- What evidence challenges it

Replace

- I know something is wrong, with
- I feel a strong sensation and my mind wants a quick explanation

Replace

- They must be judging me, with
- My body is reacting to uncertainty and I need more information

Replace

- This proves I made a mistake, with
- This is a sensation, not a conclusion

These statements help you interrupt fast thinking. When you practise them often, the loop loses strength.

INTEROCEPTION DRILLS FOR CLARITY

These drills increase your ability to detect sensations without linking them to fear.

Temperature drill

Hold one hand under warm water for ten seconds. Hold the other hand under cool water. Notice how the temperature shift creates sensation. Record it. This helps you recognise how easily your body generates internal signals unrelated to emotion.

Pressure drill

Place two fingers on your forearm. Apply light pressure. Note the sensation. Increase pressure slightly. Note the change. This helps you see how sensation varies without meaning.

Attention drill

Focus on your left foot for twenty seconds. Most people feel tingling or warmth appear. This drill shows how attention creates sensation. Craig explains that attention amplifies interoceptive feedback. When you understand this, you become less likely to treat random sensations as social signals.

Use these pages to track the moment your body speaks and the moment your mind answers. You will see patterns that shape your reactions. You will notice triggers you once ignored. You will understand the link between stress, uncertainty and internal noise. You will learn to separate sensation from story. This process increases clarity and reduces false alarms.

When you complete this workbook often, curiosity grows stronger than fear. You learn that your internal world holds structure, not chaos. You gain the ability to interpret signals without assuming threat. You build a stable pattern of awareness that will support you through social challenges, digital pressure and everyday uncertainty.

DEFINED MODELS

Understanding the Mind–Body Link

INTEROCEPTION PATHWAY

This list shows how a sensation travels from the body to the mind.

- Body produces a signal
- Receptors detect the change
- Signal travels through nerves
- Brainstem processes the basic information
- Insula receives the signal
- Insula labels the internal state
- Prefrontal cortex interprets the meaning

This pathway shows that the sensation forms long before the story. Craig's research supports this sequence. The diagram reminds the reader that interpretation comes last, not first.

COGNITIVE BIAS LOOP

This list explains how the mind creates meaning from limited information.

- Sensation appears
- Mind seeks explanation
- Fast thinking provides a quick story
- Emotion forms around the story
- Emotion strengthens belief
- Belief shapes behaviour

- Behaviour increases anxiety
- Anxiety increases attention to sensation

The loop returns to the start. Kahneman and Ariely describe these fast thinking errors. The diagram shows how the loop repeats until the person interrupts it.

SOCIAL THREAT DETECTION CIRCUIT

This list shows how the brain responds to possible judgement.

- Social cue appears
- Amygdala detects possible threat
- Limbic system activates
- Stress response increases
- Body produces heat, tension or pulse changes
- Mind scans for social meaning
- Interpretation forms
- Behaviour shifts

Sapolsky and Aronson describe how the brain reacts to social risk in the same way it reacts to physical risk. The diagram shows why the body responds so quickly during uncertainty.

GOSSIP EVOLUTION MODEL

This list explains why humans treat social information as vital.

- Early human groups depend on cooperation
- Members monitor each other to maintain safety
- Gossip spreads information fast
- Reputation determines access to support
- Threats to reputation feel dangerous
- Modern environments keep the same pattern
- People treat evaluation as a survival cue

Dunbar's research shows that humans evolved to track relationships. This diagram highlights why the fear of being talked about still shapes behaviour.

SENSATION TO STORY BREAKDOWN

This list shows how a simple signal becomes a full emotional narrative.

- Step one - Body produces a sensation
- Step two - Mind notices the signal
- Step three - Fast thinking creates an explanation
- Step four - Emotion strengthens the interpretation
- Step five - Memory links the interpretation to past events
- Step six - Behaviour changes
- Step seven - New sensations appear from stress
- Step eight - The cycle repeats

This sequence of events helps show how quickly a neutral sensation becomes an emotional story. It also shows the exact point where the person can interrupt the cycle.

A SHORT HISTORY OF BURNING EARS

Now that you have reached the end of this book, you carry a clearer understanding of the idiom "Are your ears burning" than most people ever will. You have seen how a simple sensation can travel through culture, biology and psychology to become a signal we still notice today. This reflection ties those threads together in my own voice, because the meaning of the idiom becomes sharper once you understand where it came from and why it has lasted.

When I first learned that Pliny the Elder recorded the original belief, it changed the way I understood the phrase. The Romans treated the body as a social surface. A warm ear meant someone spoke your name. The right ear brought praise. The left ear carried criticism. They trusted these sensations because reputation shaped survival inside tight communities. Once I explored the research in chapters seven and eight, I realised how much of that instinct still sits inside us. We react to small signs of judgement because our social lives demand it.

As I traced the idiom through the Middle Ages, I noticed the same pattern. Rural communities depended on folklore. They needed easy explanations for sensations that arrived without warning. A burning ear gave them a story that felt safe. The story did not need evidence. It needed emotional clarity. That same clarity explains why the idiom survived long after people stopped believing in omens. A sudden sensation demands meaning. Humans fill the gap.

Writing chapter four made something else clear. The biology behind a burning ear is simple. Blood vessels widen. Heat rises. The sensation feels sharp because the ear holds thin skin and strong circulation. Yet the mind rarely accepts a biological answer first. We search for meaning long before we consider physiology. Once you understand that mechanism, you see why embarrassment became linked to the idiom. The same heat that once signalled gossip now signals social discomfort.

The cultural research in chapter fifteen strengthened this point. Chinese, Indian and African traditions repeat similar beliefs. People link heat to attention, fate or spiritual focus. The patterns match across continents. Each culture used body signals to fill blank spaces in understanding. This made me see the idiom not as a stray superstition, but as a global habit. Humans everywhere read their bodies for clues.

By the time I reached the modern material in chapters eighteen and nineteen, the idiom changed again. Digital life creates constant evaluation. Silence feels loaded. Delayed messages feel pointed. People track attention through a screen. A burning ear still triggers curiosity because the instinct behind it never faded. You have seen how FOMO, social stress and rapid interpretation deepen the urge to connect sensation with meaning. You understand why the mind does this even when the biology remains simple.

Now that you know its history, the idiom feels more honest. It captures the full journey of human interpretation. It blends ancient superstition, cultural tradition, biological fact and psychological habit. It remains alive because it reflects something true about us. We feel before we think. We interpret before we check. We search for signals of inclusion and exclusion because our brains still respond to social life as if it were vital.

I see the idiom now as a reminder of this entire pattern. When my ear warms, I do not rush to create a story. I understand that the sensation came first. The meaning comes from me. You now have the same insight. After reading this book, you can appreciate the idiom for what it always represented. A small moment where the body speaks early and the mind decides how to answer.

AUTHOR'S NOTE

This book began with a small sensation that most people ignore. A warm ear. A quick flush. A moment when the body reacts before the mind forms a thought. I followed that sensation because it felt familiar. It carried curiosity. It raised questions I could not shake. Once I learned how many cultures, histories and scientific explanations touched that single moment, I knew the idea held more depth than the simple joke people make when they ask whether your ears are burning.

Writing this book changed the way I observe my own reactions. I used to treat sudden heat, tightness or tension as vague signs of stress. Now I see the chain clearly. The sensation appears first. The interpretation arrives next. The story forms after that. Every part of this book reflects that sequence. When you understand the order, you regain control over how fast your mind jumps to conclusions.

Much of the research I included shaped my own thinking. Craig clarified the science behind interoception. Kahneman showed how quickly the mind tries to explain uncertainty. Sapolsky revealed how the body reacts to social risk as if the danger were physical. van der Kolk explained why some sensations feel sharper when old experiences influence the nervous system. These ideas helped me see how much meaning the mind layers on top of simple biology.

I wrote the cultural sections because the idiom deserved a broader frame. Once I discovered how many cultures attach meaning to heat or tingling, I realised this was not a single superstition. It was a universal pattern. Humans everywhere created stories around sudden body signals. They wanted to understand what could not be seen or heard. They used the body as a source of information long before science offered another explanation.

As I explored the modern material, I noticed how digital life intensifies everything. People monitor messages, pauses, silence and tone. They check their phone the moment a sensation appears. They fear missing something. They link physical reactions to imagined conversations. This pattern shaped entire chapters because it mirrors what many people feel but rarely discuss.

If you reached this page, you now understand the idiom in a way few people do. You have seen its history, its biology, its psychology and its cultural spread. You have seen why the instinct behind it has survived for centuries. You understand why a simple sensation can trigger such strong stories. My hope is that this book gives you the same clarity it gave me. When your body speaks, you can listen with accuracy instead of fear.

Thank you for giving this work your time and attention. If it changed the way you read your own signals, then the idea behind it has done its job.

RECOMMENDED READING

CORE READING

This list provides a person with clear steps if they want to explore the research behind this book. Each title supports a part of the mind-body link, social behaviour or cognitive interpretation. The list avoids vague claims and sticks to practical value. These works shaped the science and psychology throughout this book.

Robert Sapolsky

Behave

Why Zebras Do Not Get Ulcers

Both books explain the stress response, social threat, hormonal shifts and the biology of fear. Sapolsky's work helps readers understand why the body reacts fast and why these reactions feel personal.

Daniel Kahneman

Thinking, Fast and Slow

This book explains fast thinking, slow thinking and the mental shortcuts that shape judgement. It helps readers see why they accept quick interpretations without checking the facts.

Bessel van der Kolk

The Body Keeps the Score

This work explains how trauma alters the nervous system and why some sensations feel stronger in people with trauma histories. It gives readers insight into memory, physiology and emotional triggers.

Antonio Damasio

Descartes' Error

The Feeling of What Happens

Damasio maps the link between sensation, emotion and thought. His work explains how the brain turns internal signals into interpretation.

A. D. Craig

How Do You Feel

Craig explains interoception in clear detail. His work shows how the brain receives and interprets internal signals. He clarifies why sensations feel urgent when the nervous system carries strain.

Elliot Aronson

The Social Animal

This book helps readers understand reputation, social threat, group behaviour and the psychological cost of judgement.

Gavin de Becker

The Gift of Fear

De Becker explains genuine intuition and the difference between real threat detection and anxious guessing. His work helps readers separate true cues from internal noise.

Sherry Turkle

Reclaiming Conversation

This book covers digital habits, social overload and how technology increases pressure to interpret small cues. It explains why modern environments heighten internal signals.

Gustav Radford

Encyclopaedia of Superstitions

Radford documents cultural beliefs and bodily omens. His work helps readers see how traditions shaped interpretation long before scientific explanations existed.

James Frazer

The Golden Bough

Frazer details the history of symbolic beliefs. His work shows how humans attached meaning to body signals across centuries.

EXTENDED RECOMMENDATIONS

These titles expand understanding of the topics explored in the book.

Daniel Ariely

Predictably Irrational

Ariely explains how humans make decisions that feel logical but come from bias and emotional influence.

Matthew Lieberman

Social

This book explores the neuroscience of social behaviour and why the brain treats social pain as physical pain.

Tor Norretranders

The User Illusion

This work explains how much of human behaviour occurs before conscious awareness.

Judith Herman

Trauma and Recovery

Herman's research supports van der Kolk's work on trauma and helps readers understand long term patterns.

Joseph LeDoux

The Emotional Brain

LeDoux explains how threat detection operates at the neurological level.

Daniel Siegel

The Developing Mind

Siegel covers attachment and emotional regulation, helping readers understand how early experiences shape interpretation.

Timothy Wilson

Strangers to Ourselves

Wilson explains why much of human behaviour comes from unconscious processes that influence interpretation.

Russell T. Hurlburt and Eric Schwitzgebel

Describing Inner Experience

This book examines the difficulty of tracking internal sensations objectively.

Kelly McGonigal

The Upside of Stress

McGonigal shows how the meaning assigned to stress shapes the physical response.

Joseph Henrich

The Secret of Our Success

Henrich explains how cultural learning shaped human behaviour and interpretation across generations.

These titles support every area of this book. They expand the science behind interoception, anxiety, social behaviour and the narratives humans create around body signals. They help readers explore the subject with more depth and apply the insights to their own lives.

GLOSSARY

Anticipatory Vigilance

A state where the mind prepares for possible social threat before any real cue appears. Anticipatory vigilance increases curiosity about hidden motives and fuels FOMO when signals are unclear.

Attachment Pattern

A behavioural and emotional style formed early in life. Attachment patterns influence how people read social cues and how quickly they link sensations to fear of exclusion.

Availability Heuristic

A bias where people judge events based on examples that come to mind easily. Strong memories or past conflict can distort accuracy when interpreting sensations.

Body Noise

Neutral internal signals created by temperature shifts, hormone changes and circulation. Body noise becomes louder during stress and often gets mistaken for social information.

Cognitive Bias

A thinking error that shapes judgement. Cognitive biases influence how people form meaning during uncertainty and increase curiosity about cues that feel incomplete.

Cognitive Reframing

A method used to challenge fast interpretations. It creates space for accuracy by replacing automatic assumptions with evidence based alternatives.

Confirmation Bias

A tendency to seek information that supports an existing belief. This bias strengthens fear based interpretations and increases FOMO when people think they missed something important.

Curiosity Surge

A spike of interest that appears when the mind notices incomplete information. Curiosity surges often occur when sensations feel sudden or unexplained.

Digital Echo

A reaction where the mind treats online silence, delays or vague signals as personal. Digital echo strengthens FOMO and increases the urge to seek meaning in small cues.

Emotional Load

The emotional weight linked to a sensation or interpretation. High emotional load increases the speed and strength of misinterpretation.

Emotional Reasoning

A thinking pattern where feelings appear to be facts. Emotional reasoning pushes the mind to treat sensations as signals rather than biology.

Explanatory Habit

A personal pattern of forming meaning. Some people rely on fear based explanations. Others rely on observation. Explanatory habits shape how quickly a person misreads their own signals.

External Trigger

An event or cue outside the body that shapes interpretation. External triggers include silence, glances, tone shifts or delayed messages.

False Intuition

A reaction shaped by anxiety rather than genuine pattern recognition. False intuition feels urgent and creates strong FOMO during uncertainty.

Fear Loop

A cycle where the sensation produces fear, the fear shapes interpretation and the interpretation produces more sensation.

FOMO Drive

The internal pressure to track social information closely. FOMO drive increases when people fear they missed a conversation, signal or shift in group behaviour.

Hypervigilance

A state of increased alertness where the person monitors their environment for signs of threat. Hypervigilance amplifies body noise and increases curiosity about hidden meaning.

Illusion of Causality

A belief that two events are linked simply because they occurred near each other. This bias often appears when sensations feel sudden.

Insecurity Bias

A habit of interpreting neutral cues through fear. Insecurity bias makes small sensations feel like warnings about judgement.

Internal Trigger

A sensation that starts an emotional or cognitive reaction. Internal triggers often appear before the mind forms a conscious thought.

Interoceptive Accuracy

The ability to identify sensations clearly without attaching meaning. This skill reduces FOMO and anxiety.

Interoception

The ability to sense internal bodily signals such as heat, tension or pulse changes. Interoception forms the starting point for interpretation.

Interpretation Drift

A gradual shift where a sensation gains emotional meaning over time. Interpretation drift forms when the same explanation repeats often enough.

Micro Threat

A small cue that feels significant. These cues produce quick reactions because they suggest possible judgement.

Narrative Instinct

The mind's drive to produce an immediate explanation. This instinct helps avoid uncertainty but increases the chance of inaccurate stories.

Parasocial Sensitivity

A tendency to attach meaning to one sided or indirect cues. Parasocial sensitivity increases FOMO during digital interactions.

Pattern Seeking

The mind's tendency to create order from scattered details. Pattern seeking helps detect real threat but also increases the chance of misreading sensations.

Rejection Sensitivity

A heightened response to possible rejection. This sensitivity increases emotional load during small interactions.

Relevance Tracking

The mental activity where people check their social importance. Relevance tracking increases during uncertainty and fuels FOMO when signals feel unclear.

Signal Amplification

An increase in sensitivity caused by stress or fatigue. Amplification makes neutral sensations feel urgent.

Social Monitoring

The habit of tracking others for signs of acceptance or exclusion. Humans rely on social monitoring because reputation shaped survival in early groups.

Social Threat

Any cue that suggests possible judgement or loss of standing. The brain reacts to social threat in ways similar to physical threat.

Somatic Echo

A sensation linked to old emotional memory. Somatic echoes trigger strong reactions because they feel familiar.

Somatic Marker

A physical cue that influences decision making. Somatic markers help guide choices but can mislead when anxiety is high.

Somatic Misinterpretation

Assigning emotional or social meaning to neutral physical sensations. This pattern forms the core of many anxiety loops.

Stress Response

The body's biological reaction to strain. It includes hormone release, quick breathing and changes in temperature.

Threat Response

The body's automatic reaction to possible danger. It includes increased pulse, muscle tension and faster attention shifts.

Trigger Anticipation

The urge to scan for signs of threat before they occur. Trigger anticipation increases anxiety and FOMO during social uncertainty.

REFERENCES

Ariely, Dan. Predictably Irrational. HarperCollins.

Craig, A. D. How Do You Feel. Princeton University Press.

Damasio, Antonio. Descartes' Error. Vintage.

Damasio, Antonio. The Feeling of What Happens. Vintage.

De Becker, Gavin. The Gift of Fear. Little, Brown and Company.

Dunbar, Robin. Grooming, Gossip, and the Evolution of Language. Faber and Faber.

Frazer, James. The Golden Bough. Oxford University Press.

Herman, Judith. Trauma and Recovery. Basic Books.

LeDoux, Joseph. The Emotional Brain. Simon and Schuster.

Lieberman, Matthew. Social. Crown.

McGonigal, Kelly. The Upside of Stress. Avery.

Norretranders, Tor. The User Illusion. Penguin.

Radford, E. Encyclopaedia of Superstitions. Hutchinson.

Sapolsky, Robert. Behave. Penguin Press.

Sapolsky, Robert. Why Zebras Do Not Get Ulcers. Henry Holt.

Siegel, Daniel. The Developing Mind. Guilford Press.

Turkle, Sherry. Reclaiming Conversation. Penguin Press.

Wilson, Timothy. Strangers to Ourselves. Belknap Press.

Jason A. Solomon, B.Ed

www.ingramcontent.com/pod-product-compliance
Lightning Source LLC
Chambersburg PA
CBHW030234170426
43201CB00006B/213